Praise for "Climber's Guide to North Idaho"

"Thaddeus Laird has opened the door to a climbing region only a handful of adventurous souls have been privileged to enjoy. It's an area of remote peaks, high mountain lakes, grizzly bears, vine alder bushwhacks, mosquitoes, sudden lightning storms and serpentine hand cracks slicing Selkirk granite. Welcome to our world."

–John Roskelley
Mount Everest veteran, author, photographer and lecturer

"Author Thaddeus Laird's new guide updates forgotten and out-of-print route information and reminds climbers of the wondrous granite faces hidden in North Idaho's fabulous back- and front-country. Additionally Laird's new book offers a tantalizing list of new lines to explore in the Selkirk and Cabinet backcountry."

–Randall Green
Author of "Idaho Rock" and "Rock Climbing Montana" and co-author of "Bugaboo Rock"

Happy Climbing!!
—Thad

Climber's Guide
to North Idaho

and the Cabinet Wilderness

Thaddeus Laird

KEOKEE
BOOKS
▲▲▲▲▲▲▲▲▲▲▲▲▲▲

Sandpoint, Idaho

Cover photo: Carl Diedrich climbs Free Friends on Chimney Rock. Back cover photo: Two climbers stand victoriously on Chimney Rock. Photos by Woods Wheatcroft.

Keokee Books is an imprint of Keokee Co. Publishing, Inc.

Keokee Co. Publishing, Inc.
P.O. Box 722
Sandpoint, Idaho 83864
(208) 263-3573
www.keokeebooks.com

First printing 2007
Printed in the United States of America

Publisher's Cataloging-in-Publication Data

Laird, Thaddeus, 1975-
Climber's guide to north idaho and the cabinet wilderness / Thaddeus Laird
        Includes indexes.
        p.   cm.
        1. Rock Climbing–Idaho–Guides. 2. Rock Climbing–Cabinet Mountains
Wilderness (Montana)–Guides. 3. Mountaineering–Idaho–Guides.
4. Mountaineering–Cabinet Mountains Wilderness (Montana)–Guides.
I. Title.
796.522–dc21   2007
ISBN 978-1-879628-30-4

Parts of Section IV: Honorable Mentions of the present work appeared in a different version in "Idaho Rock" published by Mountaineers Books (1987): 45-55. © 1987 by Randall Green.

For Paulsy: Your motivation and spirit made this book possible.

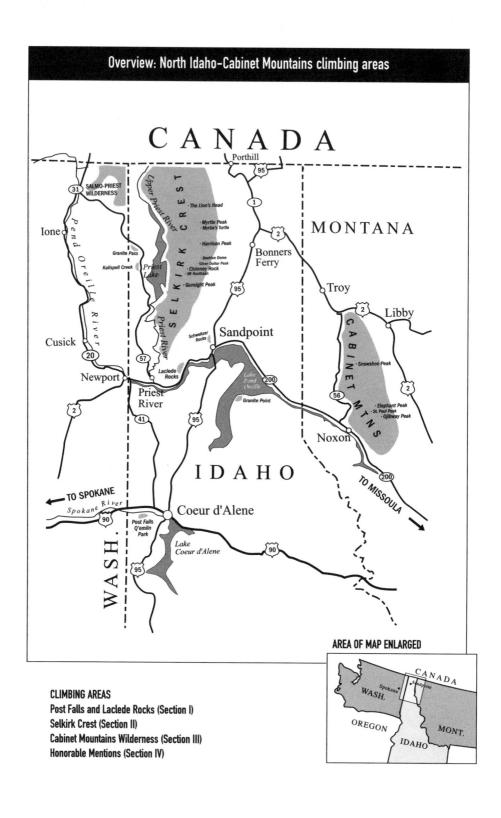

Overview: North Idaho-Cabinet Mountains climbing areas

CANADA

Porthill

CANADA

MONTANA

SALMO-PRIEST
WILDERNESS

Upper Priest River

SELKIRK CREST

· The Lion's Head

· Myrtle Peak
· Myrtle's Turtle

· Harrison Peak

Ione

Bonners
Ferry

Pend Oreille River

Granite Pass

Kalispell Creek

Priest
Lake

· Beehive Dome
· Silver Dollar Peak
· Chimney Rock
· Mt Roothaan

· Gunsight Peak

Troy

Libby

CABINET MTNS

Cusick

Priest River

Schweitzer
Rocks

Sandpoint

· Snowshoe Peak

Newport

Laclede
Rocks

Lake
Pend
Oreille

Priest
River

Granite Point

· Elephant Peak
· St. Paul Peak
· Ojibway Peak

Noxon

IDAHO

TO MISSOULA

TO SPOKANE

Spokane River

Coeur d'Alene

WASH.

Post Falls
Q'emiln
Park

Lake
Coeur d'Alene

AREA OF MAP ENLARGED

CANADA

Spokane Sandpoint

WASH.

OREGON

MONT.

IDAHO

CLIMBING AREAS
Post Falls and Laclede Rocks (Section I)
Selkirk Crest (Section II)
Cabinet Mountains Wilderness (Section III)
Honorable Mentions (Section IV)

Contents

Section I: The Crags

Section II: The Selkirk Crest

Section III: The Cabinet Mountains Wilderness

Section IV: Honorable Mentions

Appendixes

Glossary

Indexes

Thad Laird climbs the South Nose Exit (5.9+) on Chimney Rock on the Selkirk Crest in North Idaho.

Acknowledgments

As with any big writing project, the chances of one person gathering all the information by himself is simply ludicrous. Not only did I "stand on the shoulders of giants" (namely Randall Green, John Roskelley and others), but I employed friends, climbing buddies, girlfriends, ex-girlfriends and even total strangers to help me with this project. Whether it was getting a belay while I scrubbed a route at Laclede or seeking partners for assaults on Chimney Rock, so many people have helped me with this book.

It is also ludicrous to try to thank each and every person involved. However, I will give it my best shot. First and foremost, I would like to thank Paul and Johanna Haraf, my two excellent friends and former housemates. Your love for the mountains was such an incredible motivating factor in my climbing career in North Idaho and western Montana. I will forever cherish our memories and adventures together.

Secondly, I would like to thank my ex-girlfriend and ex-climbing partner, Juli Russell. Despite Juli's terror of rock climbing, she accompanied me on many hair-brained trips into the Selkirk and Cabinet ranges. I will forever remember the time we were awakened at 3 a.m., convinced that a grizzly bear was outside our tent – sniffing and grunting and pawing at the dirt two yards from our heads. I will always remember the hushed but frantic tone in my voice when I asked Juli to please hand me my pocketknife from the tent vestibule (a tiny, 2-inch blade that probably would have provoked a mauling rather than defended against it). And I will, of course, always remember the pounding laughter that leapt from our lips the moment I dashed from the tent (quite heroically, I just might add), wielding the insignificant little pocketknife, only to find a juvenile doe staring back at me in the incandescent ray of my headlamp. Good times, Juli. Good times.

Thirdly, I would like to thank my excellent friend, Bill Kish, who was always up for an adventure, even if it meant that I had to lead every pitch. Bill's strength and companionship are what made climbing many of these routes possible. I will forever remember climbing the Northeast Arête on St. Paul Peak, as well as the East Buttress on The Lion's Head. And of course, all those sunny spring days spent skiing in the Schweitzer backcountry.

Additionally, and in no particular order, I would like to thank Jared Douglas (aka the Milk Man) for his ability always to bail on me at the last minute but still somehow convince me to remain his friend. I will always remember our marathon car-to-car blitz of the South Ridge of Elephant Peak and the free beers and Patron Silvers he used to feed me at that Mexican joint in downtown Sandpoint.

Thanks to Jason Munzke for letting me stay in his house, tend the garden and get a few last-minute photos I had failed to get myself. Tyson Crowder and Arlene Aranda for solid friendship and for belaying while I scrubbed routes and knocked lichen into their eyes. Maria Munoz for being the most motivated and determined rock climber I have ever met. Chris and Cassandra Ankney for their enduring friendship, kindness and hospitality. Kurt for his wicked boulder problems at Paul's indoor gym. John Malloy for his ability to always make me shoot noodles out my nose with some offhand comment about Beavis and Butthead. And Sandy Choi for her keen ability to pull me away from this project and actually go rock climbing.

Lastly, I would like to thank all the people over at Keokee Publishing, namely Chris Bessler, Laura White, Billie Jean Plaster, Dick "Breadfruit" Wentz, and of course, Carole Eldridge, the best desk neighbor a guy could ask for.

To everyone mentioned here (and all those I forgot about!), thank you so much for your help, support, kindness and love over the years. This book would never have happened if it weren't for you.

Foreword

By Randall Green
Author of "Idaho Rock"

Author's note: In 1987, Randall Green – a vivacious climber and guidebook writer who now lives in Helena, Montana – authored a small publication on rock climbing in North Idaho called "Idaho Rock" (The Mountaineers, 1987). Randall was, and still is, an authority on the early years of climbing in this region. His love of North Idaho, coupled with his desire to support further documentation of climbing routes here, has been a major motivating factor behind this guidebook. The author truly thanks Randall for his invaluable information.

•••

Jim Wilson, a sage economic theorist, friend and climber, once told me, "If you're not living on the edge, you're taking up too much space." I've always taken that statement to be sort of a climber's creed, if not a statement on the economic status of most dirtbag climbers, or climbers who attempt to pass as business people. Priorities of more pitches than paychecks notwithstanding, I've lived up to that creed more often than not. And it all started for me at the Schweitzer Practice Rocks near Sandpoint, Idaho.

Although 30-plus years of living on the edge as a climber has tempered my space needs and risk tolerances, it hasn't dimmed memories of my formative years in North Idaho. I can still feel the sting of lichen chips mixed with sweat in my eyes; the raw, exposed flesh on the backs of my hands, knuckles and fingertips from sharp crystals; mosquito and no-see-um bites too numerous to scratch; muscles cramping from hours of steep and strenuous jamming; exhaustion from bushwhacking through devil's club and alder thickets with heavy packs. And I can remember the first time I stood on top of that granite blade on the Selkirk Crest called Chimney Rock. It was a classic, first-timer's, rock-wrestling ascent up the Rappel Chimney (5.6). It was the summer of 1980 and I was with Joe Bensen, an accomplished climber, mountaineer and photographer. Joe was my rope-mate on many Chimney Rock classics. He died while attempting a climb on Mount Ushba in the Caucasus Range in July 2001. And I miss him.

Thinking of Joe, I can't help but remember summer mornings living on the edge while skimming across Lake Pend Oreille with Terry Jensen at the helm of a Semi-Floater on our way to Granite Point, and undoubtedly another adventure. The boat leaked, and we often worried more about losing our precious racks to the bottom of the lake than climbing the steep granite.

Thinking back on Chimney Rock, my muscles twitch as I recall liebacking the thin, iron-hard edge of John Roskelley's test piece, Magnum Force (5.10b). It was August 1985 and I was with Rod Gibbons. We had just climbed a new, lower pitch, connecting the lower East Face to the Magnum Force Ledge and were pumped on adrenaline, which was likely the fuel that got me up the route. The physical sensations combined with the setting and companionship cannot be easily described, yet the memories are as fresh today as they were then. We sat on the nearly flat summit area and looked out over Priest Lake to the west and the endless, timber-covered mountain ranges to the east. The

Selkirk Crest wandered northward, bear grass flowers stood taller than a man, grizzly bear tracks left in a receding snowbank angled around a talus slope, and huckleberries hung thick and heavy in the forest shadows. The world was at our feet, the possibilities endless and our imaginations boundless.

Guidebooks can give you the "beta," the recommended gear and the ratings. But guidebooks cannot give you the memories until you've experienced the place, the stone, the route and the people that make up those memories. My introduction to the true sport of technical climbing began on the lichen-and-moss-covered outcrops of granite near Sandpoint, Idaho, with Vance Lemley and Joe Bensen. The routes were unclimbed, dirty, steep and exhilarating. My climbing partners became lifelong friends. We shared ropes on first ascents and read poetry on the summits. The place, the rock and the people all left an indelible mark on my soul.

The crags of North Idaho were the training grounds for our boundless energy and a stimulus for grandiose plans and tick lists. At Chimney Rock I followed the footsteps of legends such as Fred Beckey, Ed Cooper and John Roskelley. Others, too, especially from Spokane – Gary Oka, Hillary Bates, Ron Burgner, Chris Kopczynski, Kim Momb and Larry Peterman – all played significant roles in developing new routes in North Idaho. I was lucky to have climbed with the regional trendsetters of the late 1970s and 1980s: Dane Burns was gracious enough to drag me along on a linkup of Illusions (5.11a) and Free Friends (5.10c) and many other routes; Dane, Dave Fulton and I climbed new pitches together on Chimney Rock in 1986; Gene Klein and I looked into the Eye of the Tiger (5.11a); Karl Berkenkamp and I revelled in the moment on It Ain't Hay (5.9); Vance Lemley and I jammed and liebacked our way up Sticky Fingers (5.10d), Fun Roof (5.10b) and the classic Cooper-Hiser (5.9) countless times; my lovely girlfriend and soon-to-be wife, Theresa DeLorenzo, assisted me in adding the Variation to Canary Legs (5.10b), on her way to what must have been her 10th trip or more up to Chimney Rock's summit with me; Martin McBirney schooled me in hard crack techniques on White Lightning (5.11+) and Lord Greystoke (5.11b). We went to Yosemite, the North Cascades, the Bugaboos, Squamish, Leavenworth, Devil's Tower and the desert Southwest. But we kept coming back to these scruffy crags and ridgetop spires to live on the edge among a little slice of paradise.

Generations before us had done the same, returning with glory and defeat from some of the biggest peaks and toughest faces in the world. I used to say to my friends from Colorado who thought they knew how to ski, "After a winter of Pend Oreille premix, you could ski anything and anywhere." That's how the climbing is in North Idaho – similar analogy. If you can do the routes here, you can climb in Yosemite or the Bugaboos, Squamish or the Bitterroot. And you won't mind if it rains, or when the bugs and ticks bite, or your knees and hands get skinned up on the sharp rock. Because a climbing experience in North Idaho rock has it all – except the crowds. You can still find an unclimbed line on the many faces and peaks of the Selkirk Crest or at Granite Point, just a short boat trip across Lake Pend Oreille; it likely will be similar to what we experienced 30 years ago. Climbing in North Idaho can be unique. And while you are out there living on the edge, don't forget to enjoy the people you meet and climb with along the way. I guarantee you will come away with a treasure trove of memories, just as I have.

Introduction

By Thaddeus Laird

In the early spring of 2001, I made an interesting decision to uproot from a perfectly sound life in Seattle, Washington, and move to Sandpoint, Idaho. During my first week in town I ran into a curious fellow named Paul Haraf. Paul was young and fearless, and his appearance was made more distinctive by a patch of missing hair, which seemed to encompass the entire top of his head.

Paul was a self-declared climber. And the day after meeting him I found myself flaking a rope into the dirt below a sheer and horrendously mossy chunk of rock up at the local practice crags. Paul was at my side offering tips on survival. "Yeah man, you should totally sling that [hollow, unsubstantial and quite dangerous looking] flake up there, then run it out to that [bent and rusty] knifeblade piton. But no worries, man, it's easy. The locals call it like 5.8." I clapped the excess chalk off my hands, sighed for dramatic effect and began edging up into the unknown.

Thirty feet later, I was yelling down to Paul that he was a complete jackass, guilty of treason among the Brotherhood of Non-Sandbaggers and deserved a public beheading. I was pasted to a slippery quartz vein several yards above the rusty piton, which looked as if a kindergartner could dislodge it with a single flick of their little index finger. The only thing between a ruptured spleen and me was that one cosmetic piton and, of course, the sad little runner Paul had coached me into wrapping around the wafer flake five feet off the ground.

"You got it, bro," were the only words of encouragement I recall receiving from Paul. I made a slithery move out left, located what I thought was a delightful little foothold, placed my trembling toe on it and weighted gingerly. I was spit from the wall like a flicked cricket and traveled down through the air with thoughts of acute hip dislocation on my mind. When I came to a rest – rope stretched tight, piton intact but flexing beyond maximum capacity – I was upside down and eye level with Paul, searching for some immediate accountability for all this. "Guess you don't got it," were the only words I recall coming out of his mouth. And I vowed, right then and there, to never climb with him again.

A week later, however, I was battling through waist-deep snowpack toward an even larger chunk of rock called Harrison Peak. Paul was out front, bulldogging through the snowdrifts and calling back to me over the blare of the wind that we were almost there, that I had nothing to worry about, it was easy, the locals called it like 5.6.

As it turned out, our early-season ascent of the South Face Standard Route (II 5.7+) on Harrison Peak was pure joy. At the summit, the sky cleared and I was given my first real glimpse of the mountainous landscape that makes up a majority of North Idaho. Craggy peaks with ominous, black walls poked out from the hazy, blue horizons like drive-in movie screens. The scenic Selkirk Crest wound its way north into British Columbia, Canada. And the high, serrated summits of the distant Cabinet Mountain Range mounded up through the eastern horizon like writer's debt.

At that precise moment, I realized that I might have stumbled onto something unique here. Straddling Harrison Peak, gazing out at the interior wildness of North Idaho, I made a new vow. Chunks of choss or not, I was going to climb these peaks, weed out the good from the bad, put up new routes where possible, rake through the old ones, bring a few back to life and maybe, just maybe, re-introduce this place to its own climbing past.

Paul glanced over and noticed a fire brewing in my eyes. And he quickly began to fuel it. He described massive walls he had seen while hunting grouse in the high country in autumn. Ridgelines he had heard rumors about. Secrets that had been passed down to him by some of the tendinitisy old-timers who still roamed these hills elusively. It was out there, he urged. The unknown Shangri-la of North Idaho climbing. We could be the next generation to find it. Chris Kopczynski, John Roskelley, Randall Green: They had all been the gurus, the pioneers, the gods of this unruly landscape. They had just scraped the surface. More was out there, he mused. All we had to do was get out there and find it.

That evening, Paul had me over for baked grouse and Canadian imports. We spent the remainder of the night crouched over topographical maps, tracing contour lines with our grungy fingers and boring the hell out of Paul's lovely wife Johanna with our tales of expectant victory in the outlying mountains. I returned home that evening with a swarm of butterflies in my belly. Could this be the place I had been searching for all my life? Empty ranges and unclimbed routes? True wildness coupled with a serious absence of other climbers?

Flash forward: Three years later

Paul was 30 feet ahead of me, stabbing silently at a steep snow couloir high in the Cabinet Mountains Wilderness of western Montana. The route we were on was completely unknown to Paul and me. We had scouted it the year before and vowed to return. The only noise I could presently hear was the methodical thunk, thunk, rest, thunk, thunk, rest, of Paul's crampons biting into the firm alpine ice.

The previous years had gone by like clockwork. We had completed everything from local crag upgrading (starting by yanking out that bad piton at the "practice crags," hand-drilling a 3/8-inch bolt in its place, scrubbing it for three hours and giving it a realistic grade of 5.10a) to notable ski descents and first ascents on major peaks in the Selkirk and Cabinet ranges. We put up boulder problems in the middle of the woods that no one will ever find. We snipped trails. We bushwhacked. We took lead falls. We laughed. We soloed routes and then returned home to encourage the other one to go out and do it the very next day. We had developed an indestructible bond between us, forged in the wilds of our backyard ranges.

At about half-height, the snow couloir we were in made a dramatic dogleg to climber's left, and quickly turned into a steep, thin, classic snow gully flanked by vertical rock walls on either side: a dramatic cleft dug deep into the meat of the mountainside. Transport this route to the Washington Cascades, and it would surely grace the pages of any "Select Classics" guidebook.

Moving in tandem up the couloir, silent but on task, speaking only in short grunts or with body language, covering completely unknown ground high in the Cabinet Mountains Wilderness were highlights of my climbing career. Each decision came and went smoothly: Rest beside that wall, use just one ax through this part, move out left here, punch up to that next ledge to get a better view of what lies ahead. It was all so effortless and unique. It was a feeling every climber must strive to experience at least once in life.

The downside to this climb was that it was to be our last together on this quest to find the climbing Shangri-la of North Idaho. In less than a week, Paul was shipping out to Alaska with Carl Diedrich to free the South Buttress on the Devil's Thumb (a trip that would see success and, some time later, be written about in the 2005 *American Alpine Journal*). And I was preparing to move to Berkeley, California, to chase a girl, get a "real job" and see life from a different angle for bit. It was probably not going to be our last climb together, Paul and me. But I supposed that there was always a chance of that.

At the top of the couloir, we were confronted by a 400-foot tall headwall capped with snow cornices. We flaked out the rope and began simul-climbing fifth-class quartzite. Below us, our brand-new, 1,200-foot mixed route unfurled like a banner declaring victory.

We gained the upper summit ridge with ease and plodded along through the snowdrifts. We unroped 400 feet shy of the summit and entered a thick fog blanket that had settled in around the summit area. Sunlight filtered down through the clouds, bringing a golden wash to everything around us. I tucked in behind Paul, listening for the rhythm of his boots crunching through the snow. And quite suddenly, there was nowhere higher to climb.

As we reclined, victorious, in a sudden patch of summit sunshine, I looked over to Paul, who was casually unwrapping his signature salami, mustard and cheese sandwich and softly considering the first bite. It was impossible to foresee our futures from this point on or if our paths would ever cross again. So I decided to celebrate this little moment with a gift to Paul, something nice, something he could always remember me by. I reached down and scraped a snowball together from the slushy summit snowpack, patted it together into a good old-fashioned party pooper, sneered widely for my own amusement and tossed.

And as that ball of goo hurled through the air and Paul slowly raised that salami and cheese sandwich to his lips, everything in my world seemed to slow down to a slow-motion crawl.

I began thinking back over all our previous climbs together, and all the ones that, hopefully, still lay ahead in this climbing life of ours. Failure had always been an accepted reality of our passionate route-finding projects. But in the end, only the possibilities of success were what made any sense as to why we had done it. The places, the people, the pinnacle moments, this was all part of some bigger picture, I mused. A picture that would surely develop in the years to come.

As that snowball continued its broad arch through the air, I began to wonder what words I would need to conjure up in order to smooth things over after it splattered across Paul's serene, boyish face.

"You shoulda told me, Paulsy!!" I would dare to say.

"Told you what, [unprintable expletive]?"

"You shoulda told me that this sweet little couloir was hiding over in western Montana the entire time."

There would be a considerable pause between the time Paul accepted my words as truth and the time he stood up to come over and kick my ass. The ass-kicking would be followed by some laughter, lots of shouting and maybe even a few tears of happiness. And then, almost too quickly, we would take one last look at the mountains around us, gather up our things, turn south toward Cliff Lake and begin the long descent home. And just like that, it all would have come to an end.

Fellow climbers, the book you are holding is not merely a collection of climbing routes. It is a compilation of efforts put forth by many of my closest friends who have made climbing in this region a little better, a little nicer and a little more interesting. Thinking on it further, I suppose this isn't really a guidebook at all. It is a dedication to all those who came to this area, saw it for what it is and for what it is not, and then decided to give it everything they've got.

I realize some may protest this book, some will find error or fault in it, some will find reasons to complain, call me out on certain facts, or perhaps even chuck Malotov cocktails at my bedroom window as I try to sleep at night. The only real rebuttal I have for this stems from the time I told Paul Haraf of my intention to write this book and thereby share our information with the rest of the world. Paul listened to me intently, thought for a moment and then gave me a sincere nod, a fiery thumbs up and said, "Good luck, [unprintable expletive]." And quite frankly, that's all the endorsement a guy could ask for.

Welcome to North Idaho and western Montana. And happy climbing.

Geologic Overview: The Forming of the Purcell Trench

Somewhere between 70 million and 80 million years ago, during a time known as the Cretaceous, a massive blob of molten granite began rising (as heated blobs tend to do) toward the upper crust of the Earth. This upper crust was made up of layers of old sedimentary "belt rocks" such as sandstones, mudstones and limestones that were deposited from ancient oceans millions of years before then. As the granitic magma rose, the old belt rocks above began to break up and slide off to the east, thus making room for the persistent magma welling up beneath them. Imagine a slab of chocolate fudge brownie (the belt rocks) oozing off a mound of vanilla ice cream (the molten granite). As this movement continued, the belt rocks shifted farther and farther to the east. Eventually, a broad valley formed between the uplifting granite and the old belt rocks. Today this valley, known collectively as the Purcell Trench, lies along the Highway 95 corridor, which runs north from Sandpoint, Idaho, through Naples and Bonners Ferry and into British Columbia, Canada.

After these geologic events occurred, an Ice Age descended upon the land, and a majority of the Inland Northwest was engulfed in glacial ice. Roughly 70,000 years ago, the Purcell Trench was filled in with more than 2,000 feet of this ice. Only the very tops of today's granitic Selkirk Mountains (to the west of the trench) and the sedimentary Cabinet Mountains (to the east of the trench) poked out through the surface of this icy landscape. As the glacial ice slid south toward present-day Coeur d'Alene, Idaho, it scoured the tops of the highest rock outcropping in each range, carving out today's high-country landscapes – rounded cirques, stately ridges and steeply sided valleys – all in a place where the sea once sat.

Today's visiting rock climbers have the pleasure of climbing two very different types of rock on two parallel mountain ranges, the Selkirks and the Cabinets. The rock outcroppings and high peaks of the Selkirk Range and its foothills, which include the local crags of Laclede and Post Falls, provide solid, well-featured granite from the previously described magma upwelling, known as the Kaniksu Batholith.

The alpine peaks in the Cabinet Range are made up of the "belt rocks" that slid east off the top of the granite magma. Sedimentary in origin, these rocks contain unique deposits of a quartzite-type rock that is of interest to the rock climber. As with any alpine sedimentary rock – or any alpine rock for that matter – certain portions of it can be fractured, friable and even dangerously loose. Think Colorado or Canadian Rockies here. However, as you will find in later chapters concerning Cabinet Mountain alpine climbing, the tremendous quartzite faces, blocky ridgelines and exceptional early-spring snow gullies, coupled with subsequent summit views, make this region a must for any visiting climber.

No matter what rock type you are after, or what level of climbing challenge you seek, the North Idaho and western Montana region is a geological gem worth exploring. Walk its broad valleys and travel to its highest reaches, and you will instantly see why these are some of the most rugged, remote and strikingly beautiful mountain landscapes in the Lower 48.

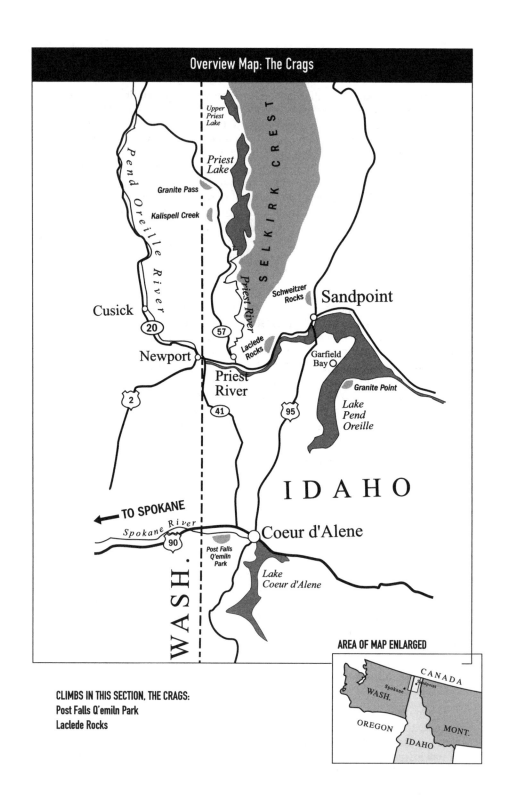

CLIMBS IN THIS SECTION, THE CRAGS:
Post Falls Q'emiln Park
Laclede Rocks

AREA OF MAP ENLARGED

Section I:

The Crags

The granite crags of North Idaho have been used as rock climbing venues for decades. Post Falls, just west of Coeur d'Alene, and Laclede, just west of Sandpoint, make up the bulk of North Idaho rock climbing areas. Post Falls is becoming known as the best moderate rock climbing venue in the entire Inland Northwest. On the other hand, Laclede, while still popular among local Sandpoint climbers, does not draw the crowds that Post Falls does. Part of this is due to Post Falls' proximity to the Spokane and Coeur d'Alene metro areas. Furthermore, Laclede has long been considered a more challenging venue with harder routes, brushier approaches and climbs where "running it out" is the standard. This said, both areas offer excellent climbing venues and tons of new route potential.

In addition to Laclede and Post Falls, several smaller areas have been included in the last section of this book – "Honorable Mentions." These crags are either old and almost forgotten or new and yet-to-be fully established. Granite Point, for example, is an excellent venue along the shores of Lake Pend Oreille. Two decades ago, this area was extremely popular. Today it goes overlooked by most climbers. It is hoped that people will rediscover the handful of excellent rock climbs there and breathe some life back into the area.

As with any guidebook, several areas have been left out so as to preserve the secretive nature of them. Additionally, several areas with access issues or private property issues were left out in this edition but may be included in further editions as access dictates.

North Idaho is a vast region with lots of rock. It is hoped that the following list acts as a catalyst for more. It is also hoped that subsequent generations will find their own little crags and share them with the rest of the Inland Northwest climbing community.

Jason Munzke climbs Freely Given on the Lower Ledge Wall at Post Falls.

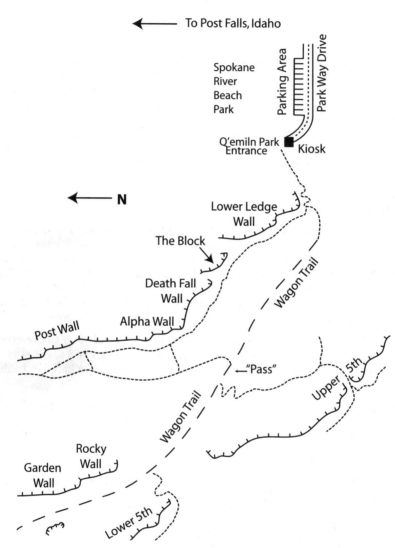

To Post Falls, Idaho

Spokane
River
Beach
Park

Parking Area

Park Way Drive

Q'emiln Park
Entrance

Kiosk

N

Lower Ledge
Wall

The Block

Death Fall
Wall

Alpha Wall

Post Wall

Wagon Trail

"Pass"

Upper 5th

Wagon Trail

Rocky
Wall

Garden
Wall

Lower 5th

Area Overview Map: Post Falls – Q'emiln Park

Post Falls Q'emiln Park

Number of Routes: 90 plus

Grade Range: 5.4 to 5.12+

Length Range: 30 feet to 90 feet

Approach Time: 5 to 20 minutes

Descent Type(s): Walk-offs, lower-offs and rappels (60-meter rope recommended but not required)

Season: Generally March through November

Map: USGS Coeur d'Alene (1:100,000-scale metric)

As with many rock climbing areas in the United States, Post Falls has seen its fair share of controversies, renaissance periods, adversarial landowners, disruption by vandals, disputes by governing land agencies, attempts at reclamation, botched expansion, finger-shaking by members of the Old School, over-bolting by members of the New School, political pressure by major hydropower corporations and, of course, climbers spending lots and lots of time there in the hot summer sun.

Climbing at the Post Falls crags, which lies within the boundaries of Q'emiln Park, goes back several decades. Folks such as the intrepid climber Chris Kopczynski showed up on the scene to establish a few scary routes that were used as practice grounds for bigger and harder climbs. Left behind were a handful of old ¼-inch pound-ins, a few thin trails snaking through the woods and a distinct "spirit of adventure" climbing ethic that continues to haunt the Inland Northwest today.

Near the turn of the millennium, hardmen such as Marty Bland (author of "Inland Northwest Rockclimbs," 2001) began climbing difficult, technical sport routes on many of the inspiring cliff faces sprinkled throughout the park. Seemingly overnight, Post Falls was pushed into the New School climbing realm where steep was king and people began developing incredible amounts of finger strength. Climbs such as Dynamic Upside Down Flake (5.12b/c), Fantastic Dynamic (5.12c), Yousted (5.12a) and numerous unnamed "projects" were added to the psyche of Post Falls. This allowed certain climbers to take their climbing skills to new levels while others (like me, for instance) were left to feel a tad disappointed that they couldn't even get off the ground.

Today, most of the efforts put forth at Post Falls have fallen onto the shoulders of the local climbing community, whose members were inspired in large part by world-class climber and mountaineer Rusty Baillie. He was part of a team including Tom Patey and Sir Chris Bonington who first climbed the East Face of the iconic rock spire The Old Man of Hoy in Great Britain in 1966, among other notable ascents. The local community has worked exhaustively to improve climbing conditions at Post Falls. By working with governing land agencies, private property owners and the Avista Corp., a regional energy company, these volunteers have addressed access issues, improved trails, scrubbed routes and initiated successful anchor replacement projects. All told, the entire Post Falls climbing scene has seen a major face-lift in recent years due to this motivated gang.

Thad Laird works the moves for a redpoint of Distractions (5.10b).

These climbers have an obvious fondness for the area and have taken it upon themselves to ensure that the Post Falls climbs stick around for future generations to enjoy. Needless to say, hats are off to Rusty Baillie and Richard LeFrancis, among many others, for their exceptional efforts in preserving this outstanding rock climbing venue.

In concert with these efforts, Baillie and LeFrancis have put out at least two known editions of a climbing guidebook devoted entirely to Post Falls and the Q'emiln Park area. Published by the Adventure Guide, a division of SeaWolf Enterprises of Coeur d'Alene, Idaho, this guide offers excellent inside information on all new route activity in the park. While there may be some discrepancies between the historic – or perhaps perceived – grades of certain climbs between Baillie's guide and this guide, both parties would probably agree that a climb's grade is relative, often personal and doesn't really matter in the grand scheme of things (i.e. living, breathing, world peace, true happiness, etc.). Just because one person feels that a certain climb deserves a certain grade doesn't mean that you (the climber) need to agree. The only thing we all need to agree upon is that this area is special to all, and that only we (the climbers) have the ability to put forth extra effort to keep it a part of the Inland Northwest climbing region.

For more information on specific climbing management techniques and current access issues facing Post Falls and the Q'emiln Park area, please refer to the latest edition of "The Northwest Passage, and Other Excellent Climbs" by Rusty Baillie.

Camping

Camping is currently not allowed within Q'emiln Park. Your best bet is to inquire about campgrounds in the towns of Post Falls or Coeur d'Alene.

Amenities

The town of Post Falls has various gas stations, restaurants, coffee shops and motels, all of which are easily accessed after a day of climbing. Spokane Street, the street used to access the crags, has numerous places to grab water, snacks and supplies.

Emergency Facilities

The nearest emergency facilities are located in Coeur d'Alene, Idaho, roughly seven miles east of the crags on Interstate 90. In summer, it may be possible to hike up to the kiosk located near the parking area and request use of a telephone.

Getting There

From Spokane, Washington, drive east on Interstate 90 for approximately 22 miles. Take the Spokane Street exit (exit No. 5) and turn right (south) onto Spokane Street. After a few blocks, Spokane Street crosses over the Spokane River. Just past the river, turn right (west) onto Park Way Drive. Proceed a few hundred yards until you see a kiosk that marks the entrance to Q'emiln Park. If you are a true dirtbag, park just prior to the kiosk on the north side of the road to avoid paying the park entrance fee.

From Coeur d'Alene, Idaho, drive west on I-90 for approximately 6.5 miles. Take the Spokane Street Exit (exit No. 5), turn left (south) onto Spokane Street and proceed as described in the directions above.

Approach

Twenty yards past the park entrance kiosk is an old roadbed (on hiker's left) that leads off into the pines. Follow this old road until it turns into a steep downhill trail with old railroad ties used as steps. Near the bottom of the steps, notice a chunk of rock on hiker's right. This is the far eastern edge of the Lower Ledge Wall. The obvious, bolted corner system capped by a roof is called The Great Controversy. If going to the Post Wall, Alpha Wall, Death Fall Wall or The Block, scramble along the base of the Lower Ledge Wall via the climber's trail. Use the Area Overview Map, page 4, at the beginning of this chapter to cross-reference specific wall locations.

To reach the Garden Wall, Rocky Wall or the Upper and Lower Fifth Canyon, continue hiking downhill from The Great Controversy through the boulder field until you pick up the Wagon Trail, which is an old, double-track wagon road that slices through the entire park. Follow the Wagon Trail for several minutes until you gain a small "pass" or high point in the trail, which should be fairly obvious even for newcomers to the area. The trail descends briefly and comes to an obvious cliff sitting directly on the trail. This is the Rocky Wall. Another hundred yards down the trail is the Garden Wall.

GARDEN WALL
TS) Tossed Salad (5.7)
O1) Organic One (5.8)
O2) Organic Two (5.8+)
O3) Organic Three (5.9)

Garden Wall/Rocky Wall Area

If you have never been to Post Falls before, or are looking for some quick moderate climbs, it is probably best to head directly to the Garden Wall/Rocky Wall area. The Garden Wall is home to a handful of classic trad lines and several excellent bolted climbs all in the 5.7 to 5.10 range. The routes are mostly straightforward and well-protected and offer a great introduction to the area. Many climbers choose to hike to the Garden Wall first and then work their way back toward the parking area, hitting various other walls along the way. Routes are described left to right as if looking up at the face, starting at the far left (north) edge of the Garden Wall.

TS) Tossed Salad (5.7) 5 bolts/chain anchor

This fun romp strings huge rails together and ends with a small, somewhat committing bulge. A great warm-up route or first lead climb, it is also frequently soloed when no one is looking.

NOTE: The next four climbs are known collectively as the Organic Gardens. They are all gear routes with bolted/chain anchors that follow interesting face moves and the occasional tricky bulge. They are great gear leads for beginner and expert alike.

O1) Organic One (5.8) Gear to 2 inches/chain anchor

The first in this series of fun gear routes, this route is located just right of Tossed Salad. Pulling through the roof is not as hard as it looks. The gear is passable but may require a quick top rope first for those not fully comfortable with placing gear on lead.

O2) Organic Two (5.8+) Gear to 2 inches/chain anchor

Worm your way up to the right-facing corner/block and make a feisty little move up over the bulge. Shorter people may need to add a grade to the climb. The gear is generally all there.

O3) Organic Three (5.9) Gear to 2 inches/chain anchor

This one splits the roof directly between the two corner systems. A little more deceptive than the other three but just as fun. Some thin gear placements are required, but good rests are generally found.

O4) Organic Four (5.8+) Gear to 2 inches/chain anchor

Climb the flake/crack down low, aiming for the left side of the detached block directly above. Pull up and around the block, gain the face above and power for the anchors.

SH) Sherman (5.9) 5 bolts/chain anchor

Voted "Best in Show" for this wall, Sherman is an old classic that provides a variety of cool moves, especially the ones right off the ground. Start down and left of the first bolt, make a fun move out right and then mantle onto a big ledge. Work up and left and finish via a brief leftward traverse to the anchor. An excellent route.

PB) Peabody (5.10a) 6 bolts/chain anchor

An excellent move through the roof leads up to another bulge and a few more opportunities for exciting displays of edging skills to the top.

GARDEN WALL
O2) Organic Two (5.8+)
O3) Organic Three (5.9)
O4) Organic Four (5.8+)
SH) Sherman (5.9)
PB) Peabody (5.10a)

SP) Spinach Free Flinty (5.10a) 4 bolts/chain anchor

The right side of the main wall is characterized by a big roof about 10 feet off the ground directly behind a tree. The leftmost route involves a fairly committing move up through the roof, past a small cave-like formation and into steep, fairly intimidating blocks above. A hair on the runout side.

ER) Eat Your Roofage (5.10c) 5 bolts/chain anchor

Just right of the above route (and slightly around the corner from the majority of other Garden Wall climbs) is a steep, blocky route that looks like it might have crappy rock but ends up being quite solid. A fun slap to a sloper marks the first series of difficulties up through the initial bulge and onto a slab, which eases only slightly the higher one climbs.

GARDEN WALL
SP) Spinach Free
Flinty (5.10a)
ER) Eat Your Roofage
(5.10c)

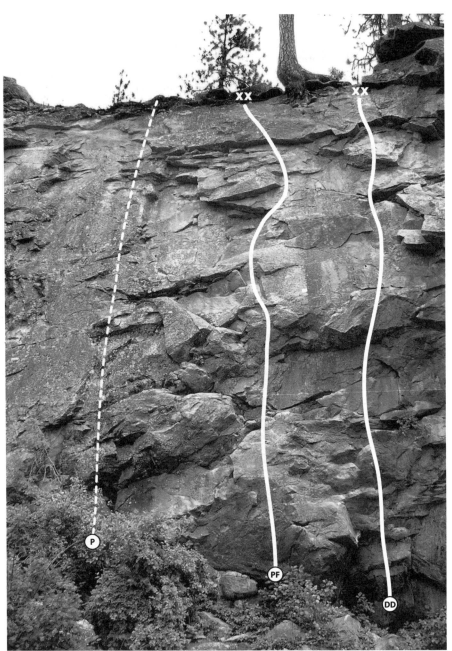

ROCKY WALL
P) Project (Unknown)
PF) Paleface (5.9)
DD) Duddly Do Right (5.10a)

Rocky Wall

This wall is actually just an extension of the Garden Wall. It sits directly on the Wagon Trail (just right, or south, of the Garden Wall) and is nearly impossible to miss while hiking down from the main entrance kiosk.

The Jagged Edge (5.11a) (Not Shown) 5 bolts/chain anchor

On the extreme left side of the wall – to the left of the grungy, broken corner – is a steep route up a blunt arête. The start is scrunchy but positive, and a few devious holds lead to the upper slab and the anchor.

PF) Paleface (5.9) 6 bolts/chain anchor

Bolted, then chopped, then re-bolted. The future of this climb is unknown, but for the time being everyone seems content with calling it a sport climb. Follow the line of bolts that ends just left of the big pine tree on top of the cliff. Some climbers find that a brief leftward traverse near the top makes the final moves to the chains easier.

DD) Duddly Do Right (5.10a) 4 bolts/chain anchor

A bouldery start leads up past interesting flakes and crimps. The route is a little devious near the top and ends just right of the tall tree on top of the cliff. A good warm-up for harder routes on this wall.

Climbers enjoy a typical sunny afternoon at Post Falls.

ROCKY WALL
DD) Duddly Do Right (5.10a)
GW) Garden Weeder (5.11c)
FL) Fearless Leader (5.11c/d)
UH) Underdog is Here (5.11c)
RY) Rocky (5.10c)
BW) Bullwinkle (5.10b)

GW) Garden Weeder (5.11c) 6 bolts/chain anchor

Just left of Fearless Leader is a line of bolts leading up through some broken terrain into juggy roofs. Move right near the top and join Fearless Leader.

FL) Fearless Leader (5.11c/d) 5 bolts/chain anchor

One of the best 5.11s at the crag, this route is popular for a good reason. A slopey sequence down low leads into a fun series of roofs. Look for the secretive in-cuts along the way.

UH) Underdog is Here (5.11c) 7 bolts/use the Fearless Leader chains

Steep, less-than-positive handholds lead up into steep, less-than-positive handholds.

RY) Rocky (5.10c) 6 bolts/chain anchor

Another heaping of classic sport climbing, this route takes the leftmost of the two cracks through the bulge. Once past the lower difficulties, punch up through a small block and onto a relatively mellow slab to the top.

BW) Bullwinkle (5.10b) 5 bolts/chain anchor

An old classic, this climb is the rightmost of the two obvious bolted cracks that split the lower bulge. A steep, pumpy start leads to a funky move up and right, past the third bolt and onto a nice slab where you can shake out your guns and saunter to the top.

Bill Kish powers through the crux sequence on The Great Controversy (5.10c).

POST WALL
MB) Mrs. Butterworth (5.10b)
JJ) Janet Jackson (5.10c)

Post Wall

At the time of this writing, the Post Wall was located in a tight grove of dark pines that offers shelter on hot days but little in the way of good vantage points for route photography. Approach the wall either by following the base of the cliffs all the way from the Lower Ledge Wall or by hiking the Wagon Trail. Once you gain the top of the small "pass" on the Wagon Trail, bear right and follow the trail down into the woods that are home to the Post Wall. Routes are described left to right looking up at the face.

Whitewater (5.10b) (Not Shown) 5 bolts/chain anchor

On the far left side of the crag is a short but sustained route on mediocre rock. Some prefer to start down and right of the bolts and boulder directly up. Either way it is a good lesson in quick decision making and efficient climbing.

The Young and the Pampered (5.10c) (Not Shown) 7 bolts/chain anchor

To the left of the big roof system on Mrs. Butterworth is a grungy corner with a line of bolts running up and to the left of it. Locate the requisite jugs to surmount the roof problem (it is common to squeak out left and bump over the roof), then cruise the face above to the anchor.

MB) Mrs. Butterworth (5.10b) 7 bolts/chain anchor

A nemesis for some, this route boasts a devious move through the huge roof, which is either dialed the first time or pawed at for hours until fatigue causes you to retreat to the ground in trembles. Go ahead, take the whipper. Scamper up the slab above the roof to the anchor on the left.

JJ) Janet Jackson (5.10c) 7 bolts/chain anchor

This is the route just to the right of Mrs. Butterworth that involves a difficult move up and over the roof, followed by rather pleasant slab climbing to the anchor above.

End Piece Goes to Night Flight (5.10a) (Not Shown) 6 bolts/chain anchor

This route is marked by a shady-looking bolt attached to a detached flake. Begin down and right of the bolt and work up past it onto the upper face. The rock becomes cleaner and less suspicious higher up. Continue directly to the top.

Big River (5.10b) (Not Shown) 6 bolts/chain anchor

Just right of End Piece is a broken prow with bolts leading up to it. Stay left of the prow. (Note: It is possible to traverse out left at about half-height to a bolt and continue directly up from there.) Finish direct to the anchor.

Frostbite (5.10a) (Not Shown) 8 bolts/chain anchor

A few yards left of Lion of the North (see next page) is a corner system with bolts on its left side. Romp up fun edges and peel out right around the roof near the top to the anchor located a few feet shy of the top. An alternative finish cuts up and left over the roof and finishes at a higher anchor. The left variation is at least 5.10 but is worth the extra effort.

POST WALL
LN) Lion of the North (5.10a)
QW) Quit Your Whining (5.9+)

LN) Lion of the North (5.10a) 6 bolts/chain anchor

This great climb has a devious move at the second bolt that will always make you think. Start on the wall just left of the broken corner system and follow the line of bolts up to the final bulge, which looks daunting from below but is made moderate with big holds.

QW) Quit Your Whining (5.9+) 6 bolts/chain anchor

There are two ways to start this climb. The bolted line coming in from the right is a much harder start (at least 5.10). If you are looking to preserve the 5.9 rating, start on the leftmost line of bolts that is best gained by using the broken

QW) Quit Your Whining (5.9+)
RT) Rolling Thunder (5.9)
BG) Billy Goat (5.8)

corner system on the left. Once on the main face, motor up to the final bulge and punch up through via good holds. An excellent and exhilarating finish.

RT) Rolling Thunder (5.9) 6 bolts/chain anchor

Just left of the red hangers on Billy Goat, locate a small roof with a bolt directly above it. This route used to trend right after the second bolt and finish as for Billy Goat. Now, the independent line of Rolling Thunder climbs directly up into a brief crack system, then pulls over a small shelf to the belay.

BG) Billy Goat (5.8) 7 bolts/chain anchor

This fun route involves tons of edging on bomber in-cuts. A fairly long route, it will invariably become known as an area classic. The hangers have been spray-painted red (in 2005) and can be used as a reference point for other climbs on this wall.

Happy slab climbing on the Alpha Wall

Alpha Wall

This wall is located just right (south) of the Post Wall or just around the corner to the left (west) of the Death Wall.

CL) Courtney Love (5.10b/c) 5 bolts/chain anchor

This excellent route climbs the rounded arête just left of the Alpha One dihedral. Great moves here involve a bit of everything: liebacking, lunges, crimps, slopers, whimpering, etc. A great adventure well worth the wait on crowded weekends.

AO) Alpha One (5.8) Gear to 3 inches/chain anchor

Begin in the obvious flake system below and right of the main dihedral. Trend left into the dihedral and climb it directly to the top. The anchor is located on the wall above the upper ledge.

ALPHA WALL
CL) Courtney Love (5.10b/c)
AO) Alpha One (5.8)

ALPHA WALL AS) A Climb Named Sue (5.8)

AS) A Climb Named Sue (5.8) 7 bolts/chain anchor

This route was probably over-bolted so as to provide a great beginner's lead. Start in a short, right-facing flake just right of the Alpha One dihedral. Scamper up the slab above via great edges and smearing. Fun, clean and destined to be a popular climb.

FR) Fredrick (5.9) 1 bolt plus gear to 3.5 inches/chain anchor

Begin in the obvious right-facing flake system behind the big tree. A few lieback moves bring you up to the single bolt. Clip the bolt and motor up to the top of the cliff via interesting face moves and creative pro.

ID) Inspiration Day (5.11-) 4 bolts/chain anchor

Start on steep edges behind the big tree and just right of the flake system on Fredrick. Follow the line of bolts to the anchor just below the top of the cliff.

BJ) Blow Job (5.7) 6 bolts/chain anchor

A newer route that can be split into two short pitches. Begin on the protruding buttress nose that defines the split between the Alpha Wall and the Death Fall Wall. Trend up and left to a ledge with a belay station on it. From here, proceed directly to the top of the cliff.

ALPHA WALL FR) Fredrick (5.9) ID) Inspiration Day (5.11-) BJ) Blow Job (5.7)

DEATH FALL WALL
DB) Death Blocks (5.7)
JU) Jude 24 (5.11a)
P) Project (Unknown)

Death Fall Wall

This towering, amphitheater-like wall is located around the corner to the right (east) of Alpha Wall and downhill and west of the Lower Ledge Wall area. If you refer to the route photos of the following routes, locating this section of intimidating cliffside should not be a problem. Routes are described left to right looking up at the face.

DB) Death Blocks (5.7) Gear to 2.5 inches/bolt anchor

On the left side of the wall, climb the line of teetering blocks that look – and are – quite loose in spots. Probably best to rap off the Death Fall chains.

JU) Jude 24 (5.11a) Mixed: 4 bolts plus gear to 2 inches/natural anchor

An old, mixed route that will probably be retro bolted some day. Begin on the steep wall just right of Death Blocks and pull up past bolts with red hangers (they were red in 2005 at least). Follow discontinuous cracks past a ledge to a final, thin crack up a steep wall that leads to the cliff top. Probably best to belay from the top and then rap off the Death Fall chains.

Bill Kish makes the clip on A Climb Named Sue (5.8).

DEATH FALL WALL
FB) Fat Boy (5.11c)
V) Variation (5.12)
DF) Death Fall (5.11d)
FL) Flusher Direct (5.11a)
DP) Dolly Parton (5.10+)

P) Project (Unknown)

This is a steep face with a few rails and bolts that appear to lead absolutely nowhere. It is uncertain if this is meant to be a cruel joke or a variation start to either of the climbs next to it.

FB) Fat Boy (5.11c) 8 bolts/bolt anchor

This strenuous route begins on the smooth, white wall with horizontal rails on it just left of Death Fall. The first two-thirds of the climb are generally unrelenting and utilize severe slopers and a few odd rests that carry the climber directly up to a large roof. Pull through the roof onto tamer terrain and follow a brief slab to the top.

DF) Death Fall (5.11d) 5 bolts/chain anchor

A harder direct start, which is labeled as V on the route photo, is possible by climbing the steep face under the overhang next to the obvious seam. Otherwise, begin by walking up the ramp to the right of the seam to the first bolt. Peel up through the bulges and continue directly to the top, ending just right of an obvious right-facing corner system above.

FL) Flusher Direct (5.11a) 5 bolts/use Death Fall anchors

The original line, simply called Flusher, finished by traversing far out right, crossing Dolly Parton and ending on the cliff top near some trees. Now, the line begins as for Death Fall but takes a direct line to the top of the cliff.

DP) Dolly Parton (5.10+) 5 bolts/bolt anchor

Located on the far right side of the wall, this climb begins under a prominent bulge/roof that looks desperately harder than 5.10. A few holds may have broken off in recent years, because the grade seems to get harder and harder. Punch through the initial bulges and then climb steep slabs to the top. It is also possible to climb a variation up and around to the right of the initial bulge. Use the Death Fall chains to rap off. Building a top rope can be tricky and requires long slings.

The Ramp (4th Class) (Not Shown) Gear/no anchor

An old slab to the right of Dolly Parton that used to be climbed by bearded men in leather boots while smoking pipes in winter, of course, as means of alpine training.

PROJECT WALL
P) Project (Unknown)
FD) Fantastic Dynamic (5.12c)
DU) Dynamic Upside Down Flake (5.12b/c)

Project Wall

This is the short, steep little wall located to the right of Death Fall Wall. Routes are described left to right as if looking up at the face.

Yousted (5.12a) (Not Shown) 4 bolts/cold shut anchor?

Bouldery and tough, this line climbs out of the lower cave and onto the steep face, past the obvious wedge-shaped pocket to the top, which is generally lunged for but rarely grabbed the first time around. You may have to use natural anchors.

Projects (Unknown) (Not Shown)

Steep and short with some odd rock and thin moves.

P) Project (Unknown)

Starts as for Fantastic Dynamic but peels out left at about half-height for an alternative finish.

FD) Fantastic Dynamic (5.12c) 7 bolts/bolt anchor

Probably the hardest route at the area. Climb up and right over the roof and then into a crimp festival that leaves most people in tears before they reach the top.

DU) Dynamic Upside Down Flake (5.12b/c) 6 bolts/bolt anchor

The name says it all. Completely inverted finger-frying along a wandery flake, which leads to the Fantastic Dynamic finish. Happy flying.

A climber boulders near the Garden Wall.

THE BLOCK
RW) Rock Whoopi (5.8)
DO) Disco (5.9+)
DT) Distractions (5.10b)

The Block

The next formation to the right (east) is called The Block. It is a squat, little crag sitting by itself in some brush. The Lower Ledge Wall is located just around the corner to its right (east). Routes are described left to right looking up at the face.

RW) Rock Whoopi (5.8) 6 bolts/chain anchor

The lower portion of this climb is easy, and then it travels into steep, crimpy terrain near the top. Take the final bulge direct to the top for added flavor. This, however, adds a point to the grade. Cheat out left to keep the 5.8 rating.

DO) Disco (5.9+) 5 bolts/chain anchor

Clip the bolt on the large block down low (somewhat contrived) and then cruise up to the obvious bulge. A few gritty moves through the bulge leads to good slab climbing above.

DT) Distractions (5.10b) Top rope or gear to 3 inches/chain anchor

The grand overhang on the right side of The Block is the epitome of "pumpy." March up the lower slabs to the major roof system and utilize the juggy, inverted flakes. Watch for rope rub if seconding or top roping. Ropes have been damaged on this climb.

Bill Kish plugs gear on Open Book (5.7).

LOWER LEDGE WALL
CM) Caveman (5.7)
FG) Freely Given (5.9)
OB) Open Book (5.7)
NB) Nubbins (5.9)

Lower Ledge Wall

This wall is home to a large concentration of high-quality routes. It is the first wall encountered when hiking in from the park entrance kiosk. Routes are described left to right looking up at the face.

CM) Caveman (5.7) 6 bolts/chain anchor

A very popular route and for good reason. The tricky bit comes right off the ground. Easier terrain leads up to a small roof with huge, white jugs and enticing exposure.

FG) Freely Given (5.9) 6 bolts/chain anchor

This climb was originally rated 5.8, which seems slightly low for this endearing classic. The tricky part comes directly off the ground. Once past this short crux move, however, the climb is mostly happy paddling on good, exposed rock. Another short crux on the upper wall leads to the chains.

OB) Open Book (5.7) Gear to 2.5 inches/chain anchor

This is the obvious dihedral on the left side of the main face. Start on the ramp below the noticeable corner. Some climbers may find the initial ramp to be a hair on the runout side. Move up into the "open book" and lieback to the top. Some suspicious rock may be encountered on this climb.

NB) Nubbins (5.9) Top rope/use the Open Book anchor

A U-shaped scoop partway up the wall just right of Open Book marks this climb. This route is fun and challenging and is usually top roped after leading Open Book. A bit polished in spots.

TC) Tree Crack (5.5) Gear to 3 inches/bolt and chain anchor

This route has been the scene of many first trad climbs over the years. Start on the easy, left-trending staircase that leads to the signature little tree. A direct finish via a reachy move through a small bulge leads to a pair of hanging chain anchors below the top. (This is harder than 5.5 however.) If you want to keep the easier grade, forego these lower anchors, move left at the tree, and wrap up and around to the right into a dirty ramp to the top.

ST) Shark's Tooth (5.10b) Top rope/bolt anchor

Similar in character to Cavity Nester but with fewer rests and more devious moves. The rock is sharp in spots and requires smearing on blank rock. The route is named for the obvious chunk of rock shaped like an incisor tooth.

CN) Cavity Nester (5.9+) Top rope/bolt anchor

To surmount blank faces on this popular top rope outing, reach up high for big rails and hollow flakes. Finish near the left side of a pointy roof at the top of the cliff. Many variations exist.

TD) The Dance (5.11c) 4 bolts/chain anchor

Thin, in-cut edges carry the climber up a very smooth slice of clean rock. Fragile tip-toeing and strenuous crimping are the techniques du jour on this dicey little bastard.

LOWER LEDGE WALL
TC) Tree Crack (5.5)
ST) Shark's Tooth (5.10b)
CN) Cavity Nester (5.9+)
TD) The Dance (5.11c)

MM) McMantle (5.11a) 4 bolts/bolt anchor

A recently added bolt has removed this climb's historic R-rating. However, some climbers may find the top to be still on the runout side. The signature mantle move at about half-height is best done via excessive swearing. A spicy, direct finish is possible, but there is no pro. Most climbers finish by trending right near the top via an obvious weakness.

MJ) McJugs (5.10a) bolts/bolt anchor

A newer route that is a bit devious for its grade. Start near the base of The Great Controversy and follow the left-trending, stair-like edges. The route crosses over McMantle at its namesake mantle move, then continues out left to a flake system. From here, move right, clip the last bolt on McMantle and proceed to the top. A direct finish exists but is harder and runout.

GC) The Great Controversy (5.10c) 4 bolts/chain anchor

Years of squabbling over the rating of this route has, fortunately, not changed the actual demeanor of the climb. It is no doubt a pumpy and thought-provoking affair that demands full attention right off the ground. Start in the major corner system capped by a small roof. Lieback up the corner and reach above for the signature rail. A heel hook may be needed to surmount the tricky mantle move. Try to make it to the anchors before the serious burn sets in. A festive onsight. Good luck.

LOWER LEDGE WALL
MM) McMantle (5.11a)
MJ) McJugs (5.10a)
GC) The Great Controversy (5.10c)

UPPER FIFTH CANYON (Left Side)
PH) Pull Your Head Out (5.11a)
PE) Peter Beater (5.10a)
P) Project (Unknown)
GB) Gyno Boy (5.10d)

Fifth Canyon

Fifth Canyon is an exciting collection of cliffs that are split into upper and lower sections. Both sections are accessed via the Wagon Trail, as well as some overland rambling. Just past the "pass" or high point in the Wagon Trail (see Area Overview Map, page 4), drop downhill a handful of yards and notice a side trail leading off to the left (south). This is the trail to the Upper Fifth Canyon. Follow this trail up and over the height of land for about 200 yards until you come to a junction marked by rock cairns. Peel right and after a few yards look for a trail leading down into the obvious canyon/ravine to your right (south). The trail leads steeply down into the ravine (the Upper Fifth Canyon). At the bottom of some steep, dusty switchbacks, peel either left or right depending on which portion of the Upper Canyon you wish to reach. The furthest east portion of cliff is known as the Right Side, and the farthest west section is known as the Left Side. Climbs are described left to right looking up at the faces.

Upper Fifth Canyon (Left Side)

The best way to access the next six climbs is to rappel in from the Peter Beater anchors.

PH) Pull Your Head Out (5.11a) 4 bolts/chain anchor

This route begins on the far left side of the face and includes a rather mungy middle section, which always seems to spit climbers off. The route needed lots of work in 2005 and may have been abandoned.

PE) Peter Beater (5.10a) 5 bolts/chain anchor

This route takes a line just left of the massive roof system on the lower portion of the face. A steep beginning leads to interesting holds through small roofs and overlaps. Move left near the top to finish.

P) Project (Unknown) No further information is known about this climb.

GB) Gyno Boy (5.10d) 7 bolts/chain anchor

This climb is located on the right-hand edge of the large roof system that spans the previous two climbs. Start under the far right side of the roof, move up past blocks and pull onto the steep, clean face above. A few tricky moves toward the top.

TM) The Mangler (5.10a) 8 bolts/bolt anchor

Located just left of Mangled Up in Blue on the steep, rounded buttress, this route travels through a bit of rock that is suspect and a few tricky sequences. Begin on the steep wall located at the base of the buttress and follow the bolts to the top. The belay anchors are set back a bit from the cliff top.

MA) Mangled Up in Blue (5.11a) 5 bolts/chain anchor

Rather steep and devious, this little number will test any climber's ability to move fast and make each move count. The route climbs the steep buttress/arête passing through overhangs and a few bits of shattered rock and finally finishes on chains located just beneath the upper lip of the cliff.

UPPER FIFTH CANYON (Left Side)
TM) The Mangler (5.10a)
MA) Mangled Up in Blue (5.11a)

Upper Fifth Canyon (Right Side)

FT) Free Taters for Out-of-Staters (5.11a) 6 bolts/chain anchor

The steep, striking buttress located behind the tall pine tree just left of Lost Arrow has, as of yet, only one pumpy climb on it. Follow the line of bolts via rails and slopers and the occasional good rest. Fight the burn to the top.

LA) Lost Arrow Spur (5.9) 7 bolts/natural anchor

A fine outing that has been a viable "right of passage" for aspiring area climbers for years. Begin just left of the obvious overhang located left of LSH. A few tricky moves lead up through the bulge and onto the clean gray slab just left of a shallow corner. Most climbers top out and belay from trees or natural gear on top, then rap off the LSH anchor.

BD) Black Diamond (5.11a) 4 bolts plus gear to 1 inch/chain

This route follows the prominent gray slab directly left of the LSH crack system. Begin as for LSH. Once past the initial bulge, move out left and follow the line of bolts straight to the anchor.

LS) LSH (5.8) Gear to 4 inches/chain anchor

This is the prominent crack in the middle of the face. Begin below the main crack system via a small rock bulge, punch up through it and follow the wide crack to the top.

SP) Spur of the Moment (5.10b) 10 bolts/chain anchor

Motor up the lower slabs just left of FSR, aiming for the shallow right-facing flake. Move past the flake and onto a slab above, which is followed directly to the top.

FS) FSR (5.11a) 11 bolts/chain anchor

Recently upgraded, this good climb begins on the ramp below and left of the wedge-shaped roof. Pull up through the bulge and onto the slab above. A rightward traverse at about mid-height avoids the stout direct finish. The final moves to the anchor are devious.

SS) Safeway Supply (5.11a) 7 bolts/chain anchor

On the far right (east) side of the wall, locate a wedge-shaped overhang that leads to a steep arête above. Safeway Supply climbs up through the overhang and onto the arête, then through a second, smaller overlap to chains partway up the face.

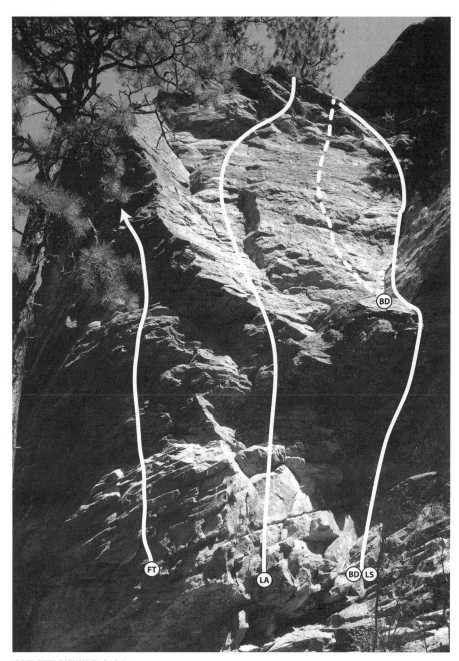

UPPER FIFTH CANYON (Right Side)
FT) Free Taters for Out-of-Staters (5.11a)
LA) Lost Arrow Spur (5.9)
BD) Black Diamond (5.11a)
LS) LSH (5.8)

UPPER FIFTH CANYON (Right Side)
SP) Spur of the Moment (5.10b)
FS) FSR (5.11a)
SS) Safeway Supply (5.11a)

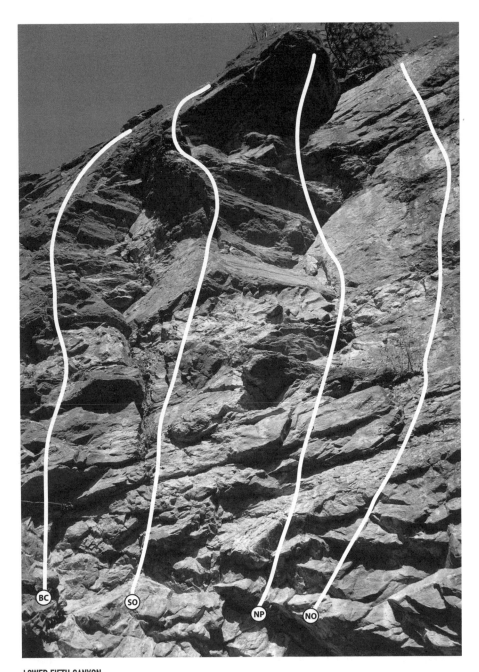

LOWER FIFTH CANYON
BC) Betty Cragger (5.8)
SO) Schizo (5.10b)
NP) The Northwest Passage (5.11a)
NO) No Pryor Experience (5.11b/c)

Lower Fifth Canyon

To reach the Lower Fifth canyon, hike the Wagon Trail as if going to the Rocky Wall/Garden Wall area. A few yards before reaching the Rocky Wall, notice a trail on the left (west) that leads down into a ravine below. Scramble down this trail a few yards and notice another side trail leading down to hiker's left (into the ravine). Note: If you miss this side trail you will eventually come to the top of the Lower Fifth Canyon cliffs. This side trail drops downhill to a short rock step with iron bars placed in it for assistance. Just past the iron bars, the trail tucks under some scruffy cliffs with bolted routes on them. (These climbs are briefly described in the last portion of this chapter.) Continue hiking past these cliffs until you come to a large, open, amphitheater-like area with several bolted routes. All routes are described left to right looking up at the face.

BC) Betty Cragger (5.8) 6 bolts/chain anchor

A good moderate, this long route is the farthest left climb and begins on a small block with a bolt directly above it. The route climbs straight up, then curves around right for a nice finish overlooking the land.

SO) Schizo (5.10b) 7 bolts/chain anchor

Another good moderate, this route begins rather oddly on broken terrain but winds up following an arête-like formation near the top. Scenic but a bit scruffy.

NP) The Northwest Passage (5.11a) 9 bolts/chain anchor

A very long and challenging route, this climb follows the intimidating line in the center of the face. Begin on smooth, overlapping granite that leads into the obvious corner systems above. Move left onto a steep headwall near the top and tackle it direct to the finish.

NO) No Pryor Experience (5.11b/c) 7 bolts/chain anchor

The large, smooth face with water streaks holds a very difficult and rewarding climb to the top of the cliff. Begin on devious slopers and rails that rise up to the broad ledge. Above the ledge, expect finger-pad edges and thin smears that lead up the gut of the face.

NOTE: The following climbs are located around the corner to the climber's right (southeast) of No Pryor Experience. As of printing, little information beyond names and grades were available.

Little Bit Rock and Roll (5.10b) (Not Shown) 9 bolts/chain anchor

Blunderbuss (5.10d) (Not Shown) 6 bolts/chain anchor

Harquebus (5.11a) (Not Shown) 7 bolts/chain anchor

Three Musketeers (5.10d) (Not Shown) 2 bolts plus gear to 2 inches

Snaphaunce (5.10c) (Not Shown) 5 bolts/use the Out of Juice anchor

Out of Juice (5.10d) (Not Shown) 4 bolts/chain anchor

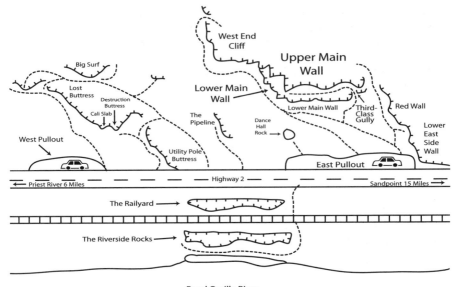

Area Overview Map: Laclede Rocks

Laclede Rocks

Number of Routes: 86 plus

Grade Range: 5.4 – 5.13+

Length Range: 30 feet to 90 feet

Approach Time: 1 to 15 minutes

Descent Types: Walk-offs, lower-offs and rappels (60-meter rope recommended)

Season: Generally April to October

Map: USGS Sandpoint (1:100,000-scale metric)

Rock climbing in North America during the 1980s was a bold and colorful time. It was a time when new inventions such as "camming units" were making free climbs up impenetrable rock faces possible. It was a time when rock climbers were often pooled together into the same category as "hippies" or "daredevils" or perhaps even "weirdos." It was a time when grown men wore pink Lycra with straight faces. And it was a time when rock climbing at Laclede Rocks was at its pinnacle. Randall Green, who, in his 1987 guidebook "Idaho Rock," describes Laclede as, "one of the best practice crag areas in northern Idaho," was a key figure in the Laclede rock climbing movement. This movement, compiled of strong, young, brave individuals such as Karl Berkenkamp, Vance Lemley, Joe Bensen, Terry Jensen, Dane Burns, Tom Applegate, Rod Gibbons, Dave Fulton, Gene Klein and many others, made it their duty to establish bold new routes, make free ascents of old Chris Kopczynski aid lines, and perform valiant battles against the daunting bush which invades the area each spring. The results of their early efforts were a handful of exciting rock climbs born from a distinct adventure-climbing ethic.

During the 1990s, however, the face of Laclede began to change. As the popularity of bolted rock climbs began to sweep the nation, Laclede found itself at the center of the "New School" sport climbing development. Strong area climbers such as Tim Chamberlain, Martin McBirney and Keith Hertel began to develop some of the blank faces on the Upper and Lower Main Walls. Climbs such as Replicant (5.12c), Changing Fortunes (5.12b), Streets of Laredo (5.12c/b), Tears in Rain (5.12a), Yield Curve (5.12a) and many others began to appear on the hostile-looking overhangs, steep slabs and thin arêtes of the area. These climbs were test pieces when they went up and will undoubtedly test the next generation of Laclede climbers.

On the more moderate end of things, the summer of 2003 saw the establishment of a small area known as the Riverside Rocks. Located down along the tranquil shores of the Pend Oreille River, the Riverside Rocks offer picturesque climbing opportunities with a short approach and an inviting body of water nearby to retreat to on nuclear-hot summer days. On one such day in June 2003, a group of area climbers including Bill Kish, Jared Douglas, Juli Russell and myself, converged at the Riverside Rocks with a generator, a drill and a simple plan: Add a few moderate, well-bolted sport routes to round off the selection of climbs Laclede had to offer. Eight hours, 12 scrub brushes and 17 bolts later, the Riverside Rocks were born. The only drawback to this pleasant venue is the appearance of graffiti, fire rings and broken beer bottles – testaments to the fact that local high school students use the Riverside Rocks for their own recreational pursuits. Regardless of this, the routes at the Riverside Rocks are fun, low-commitment adventures for the novice and jaded alike.

Additionally, the summer of 2005 saw a tiny face-lift for Laclede Rocks. Thanks in large part to the American Safe Climbing Association (www.safeclimbing.org), which donated an assortment of bolts, hangers, double-ring anchor and drill bits, the crag was given a much-needed upgrading of top anchors and face bolts. Local Laclede Ambassador Tim Chamberlain provided the electric drill and spent hours supporting the project. Many old climbs that have not seen ascents in years were scrubbed and de-weeded and brought back into the world of the living. The hope behind this effort was that a wider array of climbers will visit Laclede and carry on the tradition of stewardship here. Additionally, a few climbs that have never had top anchors (and thus were avoided by many climbers) are now equipped with such anchors to provide easier access to them. In concert with this project, a few weekends were spent snipping trails and clearing debris from the bases of routes. North Idaho is a virtual Amazon jungle of berry bushes, alders and unsightly willywhacks, and the time had come to prune back a few trails so as to offer a more inviting Laclede-climbing experience. It is hoped that future climbers will adopt this ethic and continue maintaining the area for the enjoyment of others.

The variety of route types offered at Laclede directly reflects the various renaissance periods these rocks have gone through. As a result, rock climbers looking to climb at Laclede should expect to be as diverse. A typical day at Laclede may include leading a few routes well under one's climbing ability in order to get a feel for the spirit of the rock beneath them. This might be topped by a quick romp up a desperately runout quiver festival that has you in tears while trying to locate the top anchor. All this may be be followed by a lazy afternoon of 15-foot whippers on a Martin McBirney sport route.

Whatever level of climbing you choose, it is important to remember that the Laclede Rocks need to be respected, cared for and appreciated if we want them to stay around for the next generation to enjoy. All we really need to do to accomplish this is to accept Laclede for what it is – and for what it is not – and then just show up and climb. And let us all agree that it would be best to leave the pink Lycra at home.

A Note on Bouldering

Bouldering at Laclede has historically been confined to a few small areas sprinkled throughout the crags. During the summer of 2005, however, a pair of strong local boulderers, who were tipped off by Chamberlain, began scrubbing a promising-looking, new bouldering venue called The Pipeline (see Area Overview Map, page 44). An early visit to The Pipeline found a variety of problems from long and steep to short and slabby. A few problems looked to be very classic with sit starts inside dark caves that crawl up into daylight via rails and bulges peppered with in-cuts. While The Pipeline definitely has potential, numerous hours of scrubbing and weed-trimming need to be dedicated here. It is hoped that continued sweat, motivation and development will produce what looks to be a very promising new venue for North Idaho bouldering.

Camping

Riley Creek Campground offers the closest camping to the crags. To get there, drive into the town of Laclede (located two miles east of the crags) and turn south off Highway 2 onto Riley Creek Road. Follow signs to the campground, which is located at the end of the road. In 2004, Riley Creek Campground underwent a million-dollar face-lift and offers excellent facilities as well as a superb setting along the shores of the Pend Oreille River. A pay phone, restrooms and picnic area are located here for day-use visitors. Car camping directly at the crags is not recommended and may jeopardize future access to them.

Amenities

The towns of Laclede and Priest River (located a short distance from the crags on Highway 2, east and west, respectively) offer the closest amenities to the crags. Laclede has a gas station that carries a variety of provisions including cold drinks, beer, coffee, sandwiches, canned goods and frozen foods. There is also a small neighborhood pub in Laclede. Priest River has a broader variety of amenities from grocery stores to restaurants and a few motels and bars.

Emergency Facilities

Full-service emergency facilities are located in either Sandpoint, Idaho, roughly 15 miles east of the crags, or Newport, Washington, about 12 miles west of the crags) off Highway 2. The nearest phone is located in the township of Laclede. Some cell phone reception is available at the crags.

Getting There

Laclede Rocks is located on Highway 2 approximately 15 miles west of Sandpoint, Idaho, two miles west of the actual township of Laclede and six miles east of Priest River, Idaho. If approaching via Sandpoint, follow Highway 2 west through the tiny township of Laclede until you come to a tall chunk of rock with road cuts, sitting directly beside the road on the north side of the highway. This is the lower toe of the Lower East Side Wall. Just past this wall is a large parking area (see Area Overview Map, page 44) known as the "East Pullout." If you continue driving another half mile west on Highway 2 you will find a smaller parking area known as the "West Pullout."

If approaching via Priest River or Spokane, Washington, follow Highway 2 east of Priest River for approximately six miles until you see the West Pullout on the north side of the highway. If you get to the actual township of Laclede, you have gone too far. Turn around and proceed two miles back the way you came.

East Pullout Area

The tall wall with road cuts sitting directly on Highway 2 is the lower toe of the Lower East Side Wall. This wall also marks the far east edge of the East Pullout (see map below). Thirty yards west of this wall is the start of the main climber's trail that leads to the Upper and Lower Main Walls, as well as the West End Wall. It also leads to the Red Wall and the remainder of the climbs on the Lower East Side Wall.

To reach the Upper and Lower Main Walls, as well as the West End Wall, hike the climber's trail steeply upward. After a few yards you come to a fork. Bear left and hike for about 100 yards where you should notice a side trail leading steeply uphill. This side trail leads to a third-class gully where climbs on the Upper Main Wall can be accessed. Alternatively, some people opt to climb Toy Soldier (5.7) located farther west to gain climbs on the upper tier of the Upper Main Wall.

If going to the West End Wall or other climbs on the Upper or Lower Main Walls, avoid this side trail and stay on the main trail for another four or five minutes. The first chunk of rock you come to is distinguished by a huge overhang behind an enormous pine tree with a bolted route on it. This is called Discount Window (5.11d/5.12a) and is located on the Lower Main Wall. Note: The climbs on the cliff above Discount Window, as well as a handful uphill and around the corner to the left (west), are part of the Upper Main Wall. If continuing on to the West End Wall, follow the trail past Discount Window, under the Lower Main Wall, under the far left edge of the Upper Main Wall and all the way to the farthest west chunk of rock. Refer to the route photos, as well as the Area Overview Maps, page 44 and this page. All climbs are described left to right looking up at the cliffs.

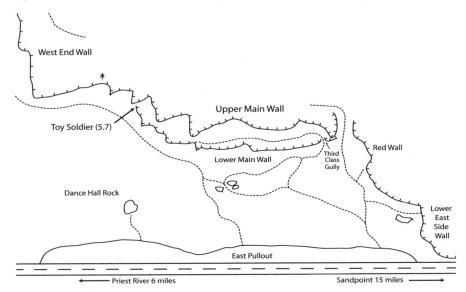

Area Overview Map: Laclede Rocks East Pullout

West End Wall

This crag is located up and around the corner to the left (west) of the Upper Main Wall. See Area Map on page 44 for specific location. All climbs are described left to right looking up at the cliffs.

LV) La Vie en Rose (5.12a) 5 bolts/chain anchor

A steep line on the far left side of the face with an obvious roof partway up. Crimp through the roof and onto the blank face above.

PK) Psycho Killer (5.11a) Gear to 3 inches/ring anchor

Due to the fact that Laclede has only a handful of good crack climbs, this route stands out as a classic. It has everything from strenuous hand jams to technical moves right off the deck, all culminating in a tricky off-balance, barn-door, fist-jam-type sequence near the top.

FT) Future Tens (5.12a) 3 bolts/chain anchor

Superb technical climbing up a gently overhanging wall. This was the first 5.12 at Laclede and is still considered a test piece. Some would agree that an extra bolt near the top would be nice.

GC) Grungy Chimney (5.5) Gear to 3 inches

For those who have a particular need to brush up on their dirty chimney climbing skills, this is your climb. Some local Laclede climbers actually speak quite highly of this climb, though it is commonly top roped.

HO) Hang Over (5.7+) Gear to 1 inch/ring anchor

Begin just right of the Grunge Chimney via a short, bouldery move over a bulge. Pull into a right-trending flake system for a few feet and then attack the face directly to the anchors located on the ledge above. Difficult to protect on lead. Commonly top roped or soloed when no one is looking.

Three Friends (5.8) (Not Shown) Gear/no anchor

Hard saying exactly where this climb is – somewhere right of Hang Over, I guess.

Lunging for the final sloper on Dope on a Slope (5.9+)

WEST END WALL
LV) La Vie en Rose (5.12a)
PK) Psycho Killer (5.11a)
FU) Future Tens (5.12a)
GC) Grungy Chimney (5.5)
HO) Hang Over (5.7+)

AF) About Face (5.10b) 3 bolts plus gear to 2 inches/ring anchor

Located downhill and to the right (east) of Hang Over, this climb is considered by some to be the best route at the crag. The route begins in a steep, right-facing flake system. Strenuous liebacking and blind cam placements lead to an airy move up and left via rails to a ledge. Once on the ledge, clip the bolt on the face and follow fun edges to the top. A variation up and right past old bolts is probably best avoided.

WEST END WALL
AF) About Face (5.10b)

UPPER MAIN WALL
TA) Threat Con Alpha (5.11a)
TR) Tears in Rain (5.12a)
OG) Organ Grinder (5.10b)
BO) Borborygmus (5.9)

Upper Main Wall

The Upper Main Wall begins around the corner to the right (east) of About Face and includes climbs that are located on the cliff rim above Toy Soldier (5.7). Some prefer to climb Toy Soldier to gain access to all routes beginning with Netscape and wrapping all the way around to the right (east), ending at Drag Queen. Others prefer to scramble up the third-class gully located on the far eastern edge of the Upper Main Wall (as described in the East Pullout Area Approaches section).

TA) Threat Con Alpha (5.11a) 7 bolts/chain anchor

The first climb on the Upper Main Wall is located downhill and right (east) of About Face. This excellent route climbs up a fun face that terminates in a smooth bulge. Squirm up and over the final hump via extreme groveling. A great climb for those looking to punch through the 5.10 barrier.

TR) Tears in Rain (5.12a) 8 bolts/chain anchor

This is the sharp, bolted arête on the upper rim of the Upper Main Wall (see route photo, facing page). The lower section is cruxy and slopey and requires a good attitude to get through. The upper face/arête is spectacular.

OG) Organ Grinder (5.10b) Gear to 3 inches/no anchor

An old trad line that seems to have been neglected in recent years. "Sandbag" is a term often used to describe it. Climb the wide crack to the right of the obvious, bolted arête on Tears in Rain.

BO) Borborygmus (5.9) 10 bolts/chain anchor

Probably the longest route at the crag, this moderate is a great introduction to the area and a great way to get to the top of the cliffs. It is recommended to use runners on some of the lower bolts to avoid rope drag higher up.

Bill Kish rappels off of The Dihedral on the Upper Main Wall.

UPPER MAIN WALL
TS) Toy Soldier (5.7)
NS) Netscape (5.10c)
ML) Model Law (5.12b)
RP) Replicant (5.12c)

SL) Streets of Laredo (5.12c/d)
SM) Sound of Machines (5.12a)
KC) Kittens and Cupcakes (5.12b)

TS) Toy Soldier (5.7) 6 bolts/chain anchor

A fun moderate involving pinches and side pulls up interesting rock. This is a popular route that can be combined with Netscape (5.10c) for a fun, two-pitch outing. Often used to gain climbs on the upper tier of the Upper Main Wall.

NS) Netscape (5.10c) 7 bolts/chain anchor

A truly wild and excellent adventure involving bits of spelunking and exposed whimpering. Begin in the obvious cave-like gash above the Toy Soldier anchor. Follow bolts up into the great dark maw. Exit the cave via a right-trending, bolt-protected crack. Trend up and right to a small pedestal and belay. A genuinely exhilarating climb.

ML) Model Law (5.12b) 7 bolts/chain anchor

Slightly contrived route just right of a wide crack/corner. Most climbers will want to use the corner for feet to surmount the crux, but the true route avoids this and uses the face itself.

RP) Replicant (5.12c) 6 bolts/chain anchor

Considered by some to be the best 5.12 at Laclede, this climb takes a dramatic line up the orange-colored, gently overhanging wall. Fun, dynamic moves via in-cuts and technical footwork are needed to repel against the burn.

SL) Streets of Laredo (5.12c/d) 7 bolts/chain anchor

A lengthy endurance event with a tough finish. It is unknown how many red-points this route has actually seen.

SM) Sound of Machines (5.12a) 5 bolts/chain anchor

This is another signature pumpy route that begins under a large overhang and pulls up into frightening crimps. Make use of the hanging belay anchor beneath the initial roof system. The climb ends at the anchor below the top of the cliff.

KC) Kittens and Cupcakes (5.12b) 7 bolts/chain anchor

Around the corner to the right (east) of Sound of Machines is a very steep route (just left of the March of Dimes dihedral). It is essential to locate a hanging belay under the roof below the route and use it for the belay. Many climbers complain that the first clip is dicey, which it is.

To reach the next series of climbs, use the cable handline located at the base of Sound of Machines.

UPPER MAIN WALL
MD) March of Dimes (5.8+)
TT) The Trial (5.12c)
SV) Soft Violins (5.12b)
PC) Poster Child (5.11d)
DD) Down's Syndrome Disco (5.10c R)

MD) March of Dimes (5.8+) Gear to 4 inches/chain anchor

This is the obvious dihedral system tucked back in the corner. Stemming skills and off-width skills are useful. The route is commonly top roped. (Note: It is possible to step left partway up the route and finish via a flake system, thus cutting the grade to about 5.7)

TT) The Trial (5.12c) 5 bolts/chain anchor

This is the steep, bolted line just right of the March of Dimes dihedral.

SV) Soft Violins (5.12b) 5 bolts/chain anchor

This is the steep, bolted line just left of Poster Child. Very sequencey moves right off the deck lead into off-balance slopers and a sudden desire never to onsight a Martin McBirney route again.

PC) Poster Child (5.11d) 4 bolts/chain anchor

Long considered the best 5.11 at the crags, this is a historic and excellent route put up in the late 1980s. Making the first clip is dangerous, so please be aware. Follow hollow-sounding jugs and flakes up through pumpy, exposed sequences. Be sure to save enough juice for the crux, which is an off-balance Gaston move near the top, followed by a dynamic reach for a thin edge and, with any luck, the anchor.

DD) Down's Syndrome Disco (5.10c R) 4 bolts/chain anchor

This route begins just right of Poster Child but wraps up and around the corner, finishing near Sirens of Titan. A few more bolts and some scrubbing might make this one a keeper.

To reach the next series of climbs use the cable handline located at the base of Poster Child.

UPPER MAIN WALL
DD) Down's Syndrome Disco (5.10c R)
ST) Sirens of Titan (Not Rated)
IN) Interceptor (Not Rated)
CF) Changing Fortunes (5.12b)
WR) Weasels Ripped My Flesh Part II (5.11c)
DI) Discrete Indiscretion (5.12b)
MB) Mano Blanco (5.12a)
MC) Mean Creatures (5.11b)
JK) Jerry's Kids (5.12b R)
CM) Chicken McNubbins (5.10c)

ST) Sirens of Titan (Not Rated)

It is unknown whether this climb has seen a true redpoint, although sightings of recent attempts have been documented. Begin under the less-than-positive-looking rock bulge and see if you can even get off the ground.

IN) Interceptor (Not Rated) Ditto to the above route.

CF) Changing Fortunes (5.12b) 5 bolts/chain anchor

A very technical climb up an old aid route. The initial bulge carries you into a right-trending crack system with pin scars. The anchor lies partway up the face.

WR) Weasels Ripped My Flesh Part II (5.11c) Bolts plus gear to 2 inches/bolt anchor

This is an old, mixed route that follows a right-angling crack. It has unfortunately gathered lichen and weeds recently and is in need of some loving. Strenuous moves through an overhanging crack system start the route. Once the crack fades, move up through technical moves and finish via a crack through the bulge to the top.

DI) Discrete Indiscretion (5.12b) 5 bolts/chain anchor

A short, bulging crack system marks the beginning of this climb. Move up and right via very thin edges. The route finishes partway up the face.

MB) Mano Blanco (5.12a) 6 bolts/chain anchor

For those who put any real effort into learning the thin sequence moves on this climb, they will probably find it to be a really fun route. Start on the left side of the obvious scoop and search for dicey holds and less-than-positive friction.

MC) Mean Creatures (5.11b) 5 bolts plus gear to 1 inch/chain anchor

Start on the right side of the obvious scoop, which leads to a slab and finishes through a short, steep headwall. Some may feel that it's a dash harder than 5.11b.

JK) Jerry's Kids (5.12b R) 6 bolts/bolt anchor

The name may be applied to the way some people feel while trying to find this route. This is an obscure, difficult-to-see route just left of Chicken McNubbins that has become quite overgrown with lichen over the years. Probably best top roped from a pair of bolts at the top.

CM) Chicken McNubbins (5.10c) 7 bolts plus gear to 1 inch/chain anchor

A rite of passage for many young Laclede climbers, this climb has become a trade route for the area. Onsight leads are harrowing and recommended for those in need of a good wake-up call. A thin flake capped by a small roof just left of The Dihedral marks the start of the route. A small TCU protects the initial moves out under the right side of the roof to a stance below the line of bolts. Tiny nubbins and friction moves bring the climber to the top. Another small cam may be used in the short corner system just below the anchor.

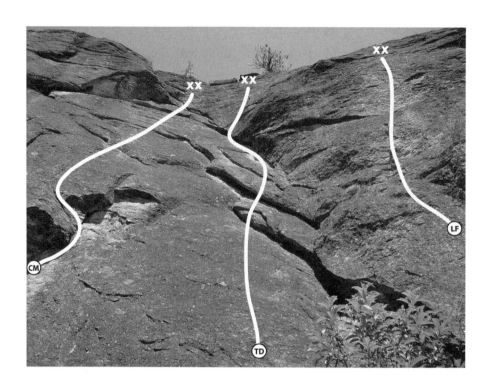

UPPER MAIN WALL
CM) Chicken McNubbins (5.10c)
TD) The Dihedral (5.9)
LF) Ledges of the Fall (5.10b)

TD) The Dihedral (5.9) 3 bolts plus gear to 2.5 inches/chain anchor

This climb is not truly a dihedral but rather a series of overlapping cracks set in a shallow corner system. Nevertheless it is an excellent route that has long been considered a trad climbing test piece for the area. Start on the line of bolts to the left of the wide crack. Work past knobs into a brief crack, which is climbed to a small, white flake. Continue up a few feet until it is possible to step out right and jam a second crack system. Delicate liebacking and stemming lead through the crux bulge and into the left-trending corner above. Just past the crux bulge, look out right onto the face and locate an old bolt. Step out of the corner to the bolt and follow face moves directly to the top. (Note: It is possible to continue via the left-trending corner system above the crux all the way to the Chicken McNubbins anchor. The moves are excellent, but the gear is not.)

LF) Ledges of the Fall (5.10b) 2 bolts plus gear to 1 inch/chain anchor

Located just right of The Dihedral, this route is characterized by a steep, shallow corner system that runs through a couple of ledges. Begin by climbing a curving crack system directly below and to the right of the bolted face. Follow the bolts to the top. The route is runout but excellent.

Bill Kish enjoys move after classic move on The Dihedral (5.9).

UPPER MAIN WALL
HN) Hornet's Nest (5.8+)
DT) Double Trouble (5.8)
DQ) Drag Queen (5.7)

HN) Hornet's Nest (5.8+) 7 bolts/chain anchor

Start this climb on the left side of the bell-shaped rock formation just right (east) of The Dihedral. After the first bolt, step across the wide gap and onto the slab to the left of it. Tip-toe up knobs to an obvious bulge (crux) with a tiny cave in it. (Beware of hornets living in the cave.) Once past the bulge, climb up to a short, steep step. Punch up through the step and follow blocky material to the top.

DT) Double Trouble (5.8) 6 bolts plus gear to 1 inch/chain anchor

Recent retro bolting by an unknown source has removed the climb's historic "R" rating. Follow the line of bolts rising up the left side of the detached, bell-shaped flake to an obvious bulge. A crux move through the bulge is followed by a knobby slab, which brings you to a horizontal flake system. Undercling the flake directly out right, then traverse back left once above it and finish through the steep blocks. It is possible (although contrived) to reach down and clip the last bolt on Hornet's Nest to protect the upper moves.

DQ) Drag Queen (5.7) Gear to 3.5 inches/use Double Trouble anchors

One time my friend Bill climbed this route and encountered the worst rope drag of his career, followed by deep patches of black lichen. The route climbs the crack on the right side of the detached, bell-shaped flake and then follows a rounded arête to the top. Could be scrubbed up and used as an actual rock climb someday.

Thad Laird climbs the route Double Trouble.

LOWER MAIN WALL
BG) Block Grant (5.12+)
YC) Yield Curve (5.12a)
DW) Discount Window (5.11d/5.12a)

Lower Main Wall

The Lower Main Wall includes all climbs to the right of Toy Soldier beginning with the massive roof system called Mother of All Battles. Please refer to the route photo of Block Grant and Yield Curve. These climbs are passed on the approach hike from the East Pullout parking area and can be used as reference points.

Mother of All Battles (Not Rated) (Not Shown) 5 bolts/chain anchor

Unfinished roof route that carries up the right inside edge of the horrendously inverted roof.

Horseshoes and Hand Grenades (5.11d) (Not Shown) 6 bolts/chain anchor

Move up past bolts, make a committing traverse out left and finish direct to the ledge above.

Another Roof (5.12 TR) (Not Shown) Top rope/chain anchor

An old route that follows the broken corner just left of Block Grant.

BG) Block Grant (5.12+) 5 bolts/chain anchor

Not much is known about this route other than it is very thin and difficult. It may have never seen a redpoint.

YC) Yield Curve (5.12a) 5 bolts/chain anchor

Sheer steepness keeps this route real clean. Another fiery crimp festival.

DW) Discount Window (5.11d/5.12a) 5 bolts/chain anchor

The overhanging chunk of rock behind the large pine tree first encountered on the approach trail from the East Pullout is called Discount Window. Stick the initial crimpy moves under the bulge and you are rewarded with a dicey face finish. Watch for "tree swing" if trying to top rope.

Weasels Ripped My Flesh Part I (5.10d) (Not Shown) Gear to 3 inches

This route seems to hold a special place in the hearts of many Laclede locals. The crack has everything from sharp flakes to insecure hand jams and a final power move up and over the top to the ledge system at the base of the Upper Main Wall. It is located in the bush to the right (east) of Discount Window.

Crap Shooter (5.10a R) (Not Shown) Gear to 2 inches

The obvious corner system to the left of Radioactive. Short and generally best avoided.

Radioactive (5.10c) (Not Shown) 3 bolts

A short, bolted route on the right side of the wide dihedral. Have fun making that first clip.

Hitchhiker (5.8) (Not Shown) Gear to 3 inches

Dirty, odd and pointless. Climb the wide, right-angling corner/crack located around to the right of the Radioactive dihedral.

LOWER MAIN WALL
SM) Shook Me (5.10b)

SM) Shook Me (5.10b) 1 bolt plus gear to 1 inch/bolt anchor

The upper portion of this climb was scrubbed in the summer of 2005 and has potentially brought it back into the world of the living. An unsung classic, this climb follows devious, slopey holds past a bolt and pulls into an excellent, right-facing flake system. Pull over the roof above and tiptoe up the knobby slab to the top.

Red Wall

From the East Pullout parking area, hike up the main climber's trail a few yards and bear right at the first fork. Hike steeply upward, passing a side trail that leads to climbs on the Lower East Side Wall. After several minutes of uphill hiking, notice a second side trail on your right (east) that terminates at a small wall tucked back in the bush. The wall is characterized by a thin finger crack called Finger Fandango (5.9).

Finger Fandango (5.9) (Not Shown) Gear to 2 inches/use Pumped Stumps anchor

This is the thin crack just left of Pumped Stumps. The first 20 feet is perhaps the finest section of finger crack at Laclede. Finger-lock up to a juggy rest, then punch up to a small, blocky step. The final – and somewhat runout – face above is steep and interesting.

Pumped Stumps (5.10b) (Not Shown) 3 bolts plus gear to 2 inches/chain anchor

This is the steep, reddish face with bolts just right of the previously mentioned finger crack. This excellent, unsung route pulls through an initial bulge (crux) via sharp, devious holds. Trend up and left on rails past a horizontal crack and then onto a short arête. Continue trending up and left, past the third bolt, on edges and flakes to the obvious ledge. A final step has you at the anchor.

Lower East Side Wall

The lower toe of this buttress sits directly on Highway 2 next to the East Pullout parking area. To gain additional climbs on the face (located uphill and around the corner from Spectator Sport), hike the main climber's trail, take a right at the first fork and hike upwards for a few yards until you see a side trail on the right (east), which leads to a broad ledge below some scruffy looking cliffs. Climbs are described left to right looking up at the face. Continuing along this ledge leads to a dead end where Jensen's Dihedral is located.

Buried Treasure (5.7) (Not Shown) Gear to 3 inches/no anchor

Climb the step-like ledge system that bears up and right from the approach ledge. The climb crosses paths with Lock Tight, but instead of finishing through the crack with the pine tree, it traverses out left and finishes up a short corner. Walk off to the west.

Lock Tight (5.10a R) (Not Shown) Gear to 3 inches/no anchor

Very outdated, this route needs someone to love it and tuck it in at night.

LOWER EAST SIDE WALL
SB) Spider Baby (5.11d/5.12a)
JD) Jensen's Dihedral (5.9+ R)

A crack with a pine tree growing in it high on the wall marks the route.

SB) Spider Baby (5.11d/5.12a) 7 bolts/chain anchor

This is the gently overhanging, bolted route that begins on the wall just left of Jensen's Dihedral. Crimp up thin edges, crossing over to the right near the top and attacking the sloping arête above.

JD) Jensen's Dihedral (5.9+ R) Gear to 2 inches/ring anchor

This is the obvious dihedral located on the far right (east) side of the ledge system below Buried Treasure, Lock Tight and Spider Baby. Cruxy, runout moves come right off the ground. At about two-thirds height, move left and undercling the obvious flake system, which crosses over Spider Baby and deposits you into a shallow corner. Follow the corner to the top.

The following climbs are located on the road cut sitting directly on Highway 2 at the East Pullout.

SS) Spectator Sport (5.8) 6 bolts/chain anchor

A good, clean slab with deceptively tricky moves, the crux of this climb comes right off the deck. Hopefully, the passing Jake brakes won't toss you off. This is one of the longest climbs at the crag.

DX) Death to Taxpayers (5.11b) 8 bolts/chain anchor

This route is technically on the road cut and is illegal to climb. However, it is pumpy and fun. Climb it at your own risk.

RK) Road Kill (5.11c) 10 bolts/chain anchor

Again, it is technically illegal to climb road cuts in North Idaho. Climbing this route puts you at risk of a ticket from The Man. However, the route is fairly popular and aptly named. It used to be a gear route that went at 5.11R/X. Think about that the next time you are top roping it.

LOWER EAST SIDE WALL
SS) Spectator Sport (5.8)
DX) Death to Taxpayers (5.11b)
RK) Road Kill (5.11c)

5.10 var.

THE RAILYARD
P) Project (Unknown)
RB) Railyard Blues (5.10c)

Dance Hall Rock

At the far left (west) end of the East Pullout, pick up an overgrown trail that leads into the woods for several hundred feet. The Dance Hall Rock is a giant, freestanding boulder with two bolted routes on it.

Project (Unknown) (Not shown) 5 bolts/chain anchor

This steadily overhanging route follows a series of flakes and finger-pad seams. No redpoints have been recorded.

Timi Cha Cha (5.11d) (Not shown) 5 bolts/chain anchor

The right-hand route with new bolts and a fierce move off the deck is awaiting a few more redpoints.

The Railyard

This crag sits directly on a pair of railroad tracks located south (toward the Pend Oreille River) of Highway 2. To get there, cross the highway at the far western edge of the East Pullout (see Area Overview Map, page 44). Step over the guard rail and follow a brief trail down through the bush, which deposits you on the tracks. Walk west along the tracks to the obvious chunk of rock that the tracks pass through.

P) Project (Unknown) Bolts/chain anchor

On the north side of the tracks is a nice-looking cliff with an obvious crack system on it. The bolted line to the left of the crack appears to be a project awaiting a redpoint. It is quite blank in spots and peters out into nothingness near the top.

RB) Railyard Blues (5.10c) Gear to 3 inches/chain anchor

This is the obvious crack on the main face above the railroad tracks. Some consider this route to be the best crack climb at Laclede. It is certainly one of the most aesthetic. Face climb up into the obvious, right-trending crack system and commit to stellar crack moves that lead into a brief finger crack directly below the anchors.

Caboose (5.10b) (Not Shown) Gear/no anchor

Located somewhere right (east) of Railyard Blues.

Locomotion (5.11c) (Not Shown) Bolts plus railroad parts/bolt anchor

Located on the south side of the railroad tracks, this route has been around for years. Utilize the metallic railroad debris right off the ground, then move up and left via fun edging.

THE RIVERSIDE ROCKS
TN) Trainspotting (5.10 a/b)
SP) Slippery Slopes (5.9+)
DS) Dope on a Slope (5.9+)
TC) Tree Crack (5.4)

The Riverside Rocks

Approach as for The Railyard (described previously), but instead of walking west along the railroad tracks, continue down the trail toward the river. Just past the tracks, the trail bends right (west) and travels through a brushy, canyon-like area before arriving at a sunny cliff face with bolts beside the river.

TN) Trainspotting (5.10 a/b) (Not Shown) 5 bolts/chain anchor

Voted "Best in Show" for the Riverside Rocks, this climb has also received votes as the best moderate sport climb at Laclede. The route is located in a "grotto" around the corner (west) of Slippery Slope. Begin on the arête below the bolt line not in the corner system to the left. Pinch the arête and bump for a slopey ledge, then pull up into the series of roofs above. The final move to the anchor is made possible by a very positive edge on the otherwise blank upper face. It is possible to scramble up slabs to the right of the route to string a top rope.

SP) Slippery Slopes (5.9+) 3 bolts/chain anchor

Similar in character to Dope on a Slope, this route is a fun outing for those looking to push their grade.

DS) Dope on a Slope (5.9+) 3 bolts/chain anchor

Slopey and pumpy, this route makes up in deviousness what it lacks in length. The route sees frequent lead falls, leading to heated discussions as to what, exactly, the grade should be. In the end, it is a fun, low-commitment affair well worth a quick romp.

TC) Tree Crack (5.4) Gear to 1 inch/use Dope on a Slope anchor

While often soloed to get to the anchors for Slippery Slope or Dope on a Slope, many novice climbers have performed their first (albeit very short) trad leads here. Climb the short, obvious crack behind the tree just right of Dope on a Slope.

Tony Glenn prepares for the crux move on Teenage Wastleland.

THE RIVERSIDE ROCKS
AP) Ants in Your Pants (5.10d)
TW) Teenage Wasteland (5.7+)

AP) Ants in Your Pants (5.10d) 5 bolts/chain anchor

This is a great route located just left of Teenage Wasteland. Power through the slopey sequence and you are psyched. Blow the moves and it will feel more like 5.11. The steep upper section is classy and positive. Most climbers opt to lower off the chains rather than top out.

TW) Teenage Wasteland (5.7+) 5 bolts/chain anchor

This is the first route on the right as you approach the rocks. An awkward, bouldery start leads to a smooth ramp, which is climbed to a short bulge. Climb directly up and over the bulge or cheat out right. Trend up and left to the bottom of a short, steep wall and attack this direct to the anchor.

Sandy Chio shows how it's done on Up and Out (5.8).

West Pullout Area

The West Pullout is located about a half mile west of the East Pullout on Highway 2. The pullout is characterized by a nice-looking cliff (close to the highway) with an obvious crack/corner on it. The corner is called New Sensations, and this chunk of rock is called the Utility Pole Buttress (see map below). At the base of this buttress is an overgrown trail that leads to the Destruction Buttress and California Slab area. Just west of the buttress about 40 yards or so, is a second trail system that takes climbers up to the Lost Buttress area. Big Surf Rock can be gained via this main trail or by hiking along Highway 2 to the east (past the Utility Pole Buttress) and approaching via overland rambling.

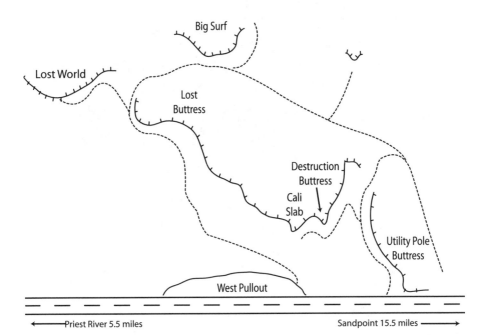

Area Overview Map: Laclede Rocks West Pullout

Big Surf Rock

Directly above the Lost Buttress, set back in the woods a bit, is a small crag with a handful of great climbs on it.

UO) Up and Out (5.8) Gear to 2 inches/no anchor

This is the obvious corner system capped by a small roof. It would be great if someone fell in love with this climb and put some anchors on it and gave it a few scrubs. The crux roof undercling is fantastic and deserves more attention from area trad climbers.

SU) Steal Your Sunshine (5.10d) 5 bolts/chain anchor

Just right of Up and Out is an excellent bolted climb. This climb has a bit of everything from a bouldery start to slopers to a pumpy flake system. It is not known who put this route up or if it has ever seen a true redpoint. It is good, clean fun, regardless.

CS) Crack a Smile (5.10a) Gear to 2 inches/chain anchor

An excellent crack route that pleads to be scrubbed and loved by someone. If cleaned, this might be the most fun trad route at Laclede.

WS) Wax Your Stick (5.11b/c) Bolts plus gear to 2 inches/chain anchor

A fun, demanding route that begins as difficult face climbing, then utilizes the right-trending flake system before exiting up and right to the top. Seems a bit hard for the grade.

BIG SURF ROCK
UO) Up and Out (5.8)
SU) Steal Your Sunshine (5.10d)
CS) Crack a Smile (5.10a)
WS) Wax Your Stick (5.11b/c)

CALIFORNIA SLAB
PH) Pacific Coast Highway (5.9)
SL) State Line (5.10b)

Lost Buttress

From the West Pullout parking area, locate the main climber's trail about 40 yards west of the Utility Pole Buttress. Take this trail steeply upward, past a few cairns and into thick trees. Continue up through the trees to the base of the buttress. The steep, white, striking route with bolts that is first encountered on the approach is called After Midnight. All subsequent routes are located around the corner to the left (west).

Jugs to Jugs (5.11) (Not Shown) Bolts plus gear to 2 inch/bolt anchor

An excellent climb, the cruxy start may have increased in difficulty over the years as a few holds seem to have broken off. This is the steep line just left of Achilles' Weakness. Endure the reachy sequences and you will be rewarded with jugs and a wild ride to the top.

Achilles' Weakness (5.10d) (Not Shown) Bolts plus gear to 2 inch/bolt anchor

Voted one of the best overall climbs at Laclede, this endearing classic is so much fun it is hard even to describe. It is located in a west-facing, amphitheater-like section of cliff, which looks, at first, to be much harder than 5.10 due to its bulging, slightly overhanging nature. The route follows the chalk marks and a few bolts up to the big ledge with the massive pine tree on it.

After Midnight (5.12a) (Not Shown) 5 bolts/chain anchor

A steep, striking route with an obvious flake system one must fondle to surmount the crux.

California Slab

From the West Pullout parking area, walk over to the base of the Utility Pole Buttress (located directly on Highway 2) and locate a thin, overgrown trail that follows the base of the cliffs in a northerly direction. Bushwhack through the woods uphill, passing a small outcrop in the trees (called the Sentinel). Eventually you come to a tall buttress with an obvious arête on it. This is the Destruction Buttress and the arête is called Sensitive Dependence (5.10c). Just left (west) of the Destruction Buttress is a protruding rock slab the shape of the State of California. This is called the California Slab. Two great climbs are located here.

PH) Pacific Coast Highway (5.9) 2 bolts plus gear to 1 inch/chain anchor

The easiest start is done by walking up the right side of the formation for a few feet and then traversing out onto the face. Continue traversing out left toward the small tree. Gear can be placed in a small crack near the base of the tree. From here, continue directly up the left side of the formation, passing a couple of bolts to the top.

SL) State Line (5.10b) 4 bolts/chain anchor

Begin as for Pacific Coast Highway. However, instead of traversing left, climb directly up the right side of the formation, utilizing the edge of the arête. An excellent route involving a little bit of everything. A wee bit runout but definitely "all there" and well worth the effort.

DESTRUCTION BUTTRESS
AZ) Arizona (5.11c/d)
SD) Sensitive Dependence (5.10c)

Destruction Buttress

Follow the approach direction for the California Slab. The Destruction Buttress is located just right (east) of this slab. It is characterized by an obvious, fairly tall arête called Sensitive Dependence (5.10c).

AZ) Arizona (5.11c/d) 4 bolts plus gear to 2 inch/chain anchor

This is the steep, reddish face to the left of the Sensitive Dependence arête. Begin by scrambling up blocks to the base of the wall. Take a direct line up through thin, sharp holds; punch through the roof and then vomit.

SD) Sensitive Dependence (5.10c) 3 bolts plus gear to 1 inch/chain anchor

This is the obvious arête on the formation (see route photo). To gain the base of the route, scramble up the right side of the crag for a few feet until it is possible to gain a small ledge directly below the first bolt. Belayer should probably clip in to the first bolt to protect himself or herself.

Edge of Destruction (5.11b) (Not Shown) Gear/chain anchor

Located somewhere among the munge to the right of Sensitive Dependence.

The Sentinel

This is the small outcrop located in shady trees uphill (north) of the Utility Pole Buttress. It is a tiny, rectangular rock formation that is normally waved at and then ignored while walking briskly toward the California Slab area.

Left Overture (5.11) (Not Shown) 2 bolts/no anchor

The only route on the Sentinel, it follows the line of bolts past an interesting dyno sequence and then gets run out near the top. Why not add a few more bolts and an anchor? Seems like an abandoned project.

UTILITY POLE BUTTRESS
NW) New Sensations (5.9)
BB) Bug Bite (5.11b)

Utility Pole Buttress

This is the roadside crag (located next to Highway 2) beside the West Pullout Area. The approach should take less than 20 seconds and offers a fun gear route and a difficult but inspiring bolted route.

Legs Over Easy (5.6) (Not Shown) Gear/no anchor

Nothing special. This is the crack system to the left of New Sensations.

NW) New Sensations (5.9) Gear to 4 inch/use Bug Bite anchor

This is a classic corner system that has been used as a training climb for years. Begin in the wide slot below the ledge below the main corner system. Paddle up the ledge, enter the corner system and motor up it. Near the top of the corner, make a rightward traverse via a flake/crack system and end at the Bug Bite anchors.

BB) Bug Bite (5.11b) 7 bolts/chain anchor

A surprisingly difficult mantle begins this excellent sport climb. Move up and left after the mantle, passing through excellent sequences. Some climbers actually go all the way to the top of New Sensations, put in a small cam and then traverse back right to the anchor. Otherwise, take the devious direct finish straight to the anchors.

The Lost World (aka Landshark Buttress, Spokane Slab, Deception Pinnacles)

Long ago, some climbers decided to put up a handful of routes on some promising chunks of rock located in the bush northwest of the Lost Buttress. However, they seem to have become disinterested as time went on. All the trails are now overgrown, lichen adorns many of the faces and even the hardware seems to be losing its battle against the oppressive North Idaho winters. Recent expeditions into the Lost World, however, have unsurfaced a few good climbs and many sections of yet-to-be-explored rock. Go get 'em!!

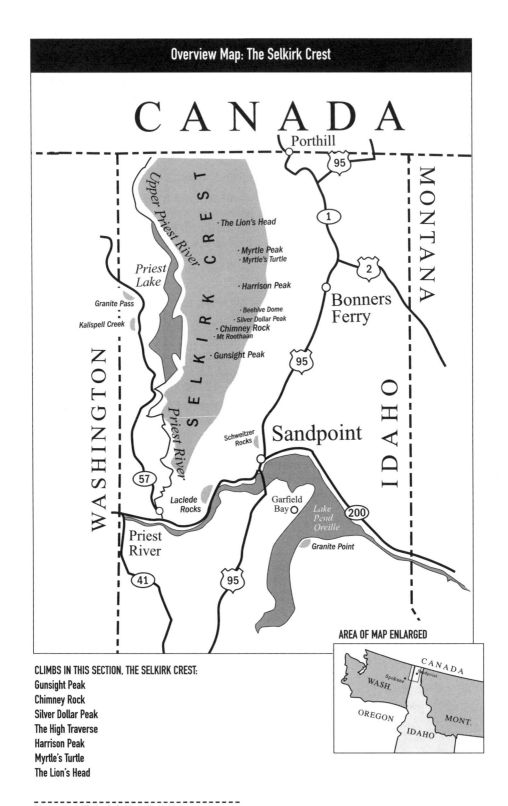

Overview Map: The Selkirk Crest

CANADA

Porthill

95

MONTANA

1

· The Lion's Head

· Myrtle Peak
· Myrtle's Turtle

2

· Harrison Peak

Bonners Ferry

· Beehive Dome
· Silver Dollar Peak
· Chimney Rock
· Mt Roothaan

· Gunsight Peak

95

Upper Priest River

Priest Lake

Granite Pass

Kalispell Creek

SELKIRK CREST

Priest River

Schweitzer Rocks

Sandpoint

IDAHO

WASHINGTON

57

Laclede Rocks

Garfield Bay O

Lake Pend Oreille

200

Priest River

41

95

Granite Point

AREA OF MAP ENLARGED

CANADA

Spokane · Sandpoint

WASH.

OREGON

MONT.

IDAHO

CLIMBS IN THIS SECTION, THE SELKIRK CREST:
Gunsight Peak
Chimney Rock
Silver Dollar Peak
The High Traverse
Harrison Peak
Myrtle's Turtle
The Lion's Head

Section II:

The Selkirk Crest

" ... There's a spirit in those who explore the Selkirks, and that spirit will recognize a kindred soul."

–John Roskelley, Himalayan veteran and former Spokane City Councilman

The rocky backbone of peaks stretching north from Schweitzer Mountain Resort all the way to the Canadian border is known collectively as the Selkirk Crest. This stretch of mountainous landscape, which includes scoured cirques, wooded ridges, alpine bowls, rock towers, ominous north-facing walls and miles of open bear grass country, are some of the most rugged and spectacular high country in the West.

According to Randall Green's "Idaho Rock," early exploration of this area was limited because access was extremely poor. Only Native Americans, fur traders, and mining and timber prospectors ventured into this remote wilderness. During the early 1900s, roads began to be built into the region to gain access to large stands of virgin timber. The logging industry has blossomed here ever since.

Not until the 1930s did explorers begin looking at the rocky summits of the Selkirk Crest as avenues for sport. Chimney Rock – clearly visible from the western shores of Priest Lake – became the first target. This solitary, free-standing summit became a destination for many Northwest climbers. As a result, the peak has quite a colorful climbing history. It was first climbed in 1934 by a team from Seattle. Today, it is widely considered to be the finest rock climbing venue in the Inland Northwest.

As with any mountain range, the Selkirks present their own list of advantages and disadvantages to the rock climber. One of its strongest attributes is its relative wildness and remoteness as compared to other such ranges in the Lower 48. This, however, means that present-day road access into the region can still be an issue.

You will find no paved roads winding up through high mountain passes like you do over in the Cascade Range or in the Rockies. Most of the roads leading into the Selkirks are Forest Service roads, which means they are often unmaintained or, at the very least, partially maintained. These spicy little roads usually present the first adventure of the day on one's approach to the Selkirk Crest. The logging industry, while often considered destructive to the surrounding natural environment, has allowed access into many parts of the Selkirks that would otherwise be impossible to reach by vehicle. As with many mountainous areas around the West, this conundrum of logging versus recreation continues to be a hot topic for regional land managers and local inhabitants. Regardless of your stance on the issues, today's visiting climbers are given far more access privileges than the pioneering climbers before us.

The general rule of thumb when exploring the Selkirks is to contact the Forest Service in Sandpoint or Priest Lake, Idaho, and get updated road conditions and closure information. Just because there was a road into a particular venue when this book was written doesn't mean it will be there in the future.

Once inside the range itself, it is obvious why so many different people choose to live, work and recreate here. And it can only be hoped that we can all work together to insure that access is never compromised into this special range. For all of you who have never had the pleasure of visiting the Selkirks before, welcome to one of the greatest, wildest places left in the Pacific Northwest.

The Selkirk Crest seen from an airplane, with Chimney Rock in the forefront and Priest Lake in the background

Photo by Doug Marshall

Gunsight Peak

Gunsight Peak (7,352 feet)

Number of Routes: Four

Grade Range: 5.8 to 5.9 A1

Length Range: 500 feet to 800 feet

Approach Time: 2.5 hours (for the North Face) and 3.5 hours (for the East Face)

Climbing Time: 3 to 7 hours

Total Elevation Gain (car to summit): 2,052 feet

Descent Type: Walk-off

Season: Generally June through late September

Maps: USGS Mount Roothaan (7.5-minute series) or USGS Bonners Ferry (1:100,000-scale metric)

Located directly on the Selkirk Crest roughly two miles south of Mount Roothaan, Gunsight Peak is characterized by broad, twin summits. Its taller North Peak has long bear grass slopes on its west side, a sweeping North Face and a steep, blocky East Face: the latter two being of interest to the alpine rock climber. The rock quality on Gunsight Peak pales in comparison to the exceptional rock found on nearby Chimney Rock. However, as on Chimney Rock, the rock on the East Face of Gunsight is better, and the setting is just as spectacular. Climbs on the North Face, however, have all but been lost to the ages. These are rarely climbed and are perhaps dangerous because of it. They have been included here for historical preservation. Climb them with caution.

Camping
Hunt Lake offers a few primitive camping spots along the lakeshore. If climbing the East Face, camping can be found at the tarn located directly below the face. See *Approach* description, page 88, for details on getting to this tarn.

Amenities
The township of Coolin has a small café/store that offers excellent shakes, burgers, a small assortment of groceries and canned goods, and pop and other beverages. Beer can be purchased for take-away at the neighboring bar. For those with extra time and a need for a real meal, drive around to the west side of Priest Lake and follow Highway 57 north to the town of Nordman.

Emergency Facilities
The closest pay phone is located in the township of Coolin. However, Newport, Washington, roughly 36 miles southwest of Coolin on Highway 2, offers the closest emergency facilities.

Getting There
From the town of Priest River, Idaho, drive north on Highway 57 for approximately 23 miles and turn right (east) toward the township of Coolin. Go about

East Face

BM RC OB

Hunt Lake

GUNSIGHT PEAK (NORTH FACE)
BM) Bergman-Miller (III 5.8 A2)
RC) Roskelley-Castle (III 5.9 R/A1)
OB) Oka-Bates (III 5.8)

5.25 miles to Coolin and turn right (east) onto Cavanaugh Bay Road. Travel another three miles or so and veer right onto East Shore Road, following this about 4.5 miles to Road No. 24 (Hunt Creek Road), which is located a few yards past a cement bridge spanning Hunt Creek. Turn onto Road 24, a dirt road, and follow it for four miles to its junction with Road 2. Bear right (staying on Road 24) and go about 1.25 miles to a fork. Go steeply to the left onto Road 241. Drive 3.5 miles farther along this rough and rutted road to the Hunt Lake trailhead.

Approach
Both the North Face and the East Face are approached via Hunt Lake. From the trailhead, boulder hop through talus for about one mile, following the spray-painted rocks to Hunt Lake. If approaching the North Face, hike the broad bear grass slopes northeast of the lake, which lead up to a ridge that separates Gunsight Peak from Mount Roothaan. From a low point in the ridge, find the path of least resistance down to the base of the North Face.

If approaching the East Face, traverse around to the southeast edge of Hunt Lake. Rising above is a talus slope littered with trees that leads to a pass just south of Gunsight Peak's South Summit (6,913 feet). From this pass, descend to the east and begin traversing in a northerly manner toward a spur ridge that tumbles off the east side of Gunsight's North Peak. Once you gain this spur ridge, notice a small tarn in the basin below (marked as 6,653 feet on the USGS Mount Roothaan map). Directly to the west above the tarn is the East Face of Gunsight Peak. Scramble up talus and rock slabs to the base of the route.

North Face (North Peak)

"Dark, dirty and foreboding" probably best describes the North Face of Gunsight Peak. Old and outdated, some routes have probably never been repeated. They were notable feats for their day and should not be lost to history. The next time you are approaching Chimney Rock via Mount Roothaan, look over at the daunting North Face of Gunsight Peak and think about the men who boldly acted on their dreams to climb it. The main face is 800 feet tall.

BM) Bergman/Miller (5.8 A2) 5 to 6 pitches

Just left of center on the main North Face, a prominent chimney/corner system runs directly from the lower talus fields to the summit. The Bergman/Miller route follows this corner system. Some aid was used on the original ascent, and the party experienced rockfall and wetness. Enjoy.

RC) Roskelley/Castle (5.9 R/A1) 5 to 6 pitches

This route, the second to be established on the face, follows the next major chimney weakness to the right (west) of Bergman/Miller. The chimney is rumored not to protect well. Roskelley reportedly led the entire route and encountered down-sloping slabs with very few points of protection.

OB) Oka/Bates (5.8) 4 pitches

A third chimney system splits the wall just right of the Roskelley/Castle route. The climb is easier than the others on the North Face, but similar issues of looseness and poor pro may be a problem. No further information is available.

East Face (North Peak)

The East Face of Gunsight Peak is a cleaner, shorter and less-formidable objective than its north-facing counterpart. The Winchester route takes a fairly direct line up the face and includes enjoyable climbing at a moderate grade. However, do not expect the East Face of this peak to be like the East Face of Chimney Rock. The rock is still suspicious in certain areas, and the low amount of traffic on the face means that detached flakes and teetering blocks are probably in need of trundling.

Winchester (5.8+) (Not Shown) 3 to 4 pitches/gear to 3 inches

Pitch 1: Begin just left of a large, detached block with orange lichen growing on its left side. Face climb up to a shallow, left-trending corner system above the detached block. Continue up steep rock to a dihedral. A tricky mantle leads up and left to a series of flakes. Climb up past a large block that is separated from the main wall and belay.

Pitch 2: Climb up to the top of a large, detached flake to an ugly, dirty roof. Skirt the roof on the right via face climbing. Continue up grooves, past a dead tree to a prominent belay ledge.

Pitch 3: Climb short steps and blocks on easier ground to the summit ridge.

Descent: Hike down McCormick Ridge, which drops away from the summit to the northeast, and wrap back around to the basin and tarn (6,653 feet). Retrace your steps back to Hunt Lake and the car.

The striking East Face of Chimney Rock

Chimney Rock

Chimney Rock (7,124 feet)

Number of Routes: 29 known

Grade Range: 5.5 to 5.11d

Length Range: 3 to 4 pitches (350 feet to 500 feet)

Approach Time: 1.5 hours (via West Approach); 3 hours (via the East Approach)

Climbing Time: 2 to 4 hours

Total Elevation Gain (car to summit): 1,033 feet (via the West Approach); 3,104 feet (via the East Approach)

Descent Type: 3 to 4 single-rope (60-meter) rappels or 2 to 3 double-rope rappels

Season: Generally June through late September

Maps: USGS Mount Roothaan (7.5-minute series) or USGS Bonners Ferry (1:100,000-scale metric)

Standing precariously on the Selkirk Crest roughly a half mile northeast of Mount Roothaan, Chimney Rock punches up through the North Idaho wilderness like an enormous mythical fist threatening the sky. This dramatic mountain feature has three main faces that are of importance to the rock climber. The 500-foot tall East Face holds the best selection of climbs, which average three pitches in length and offer strenuous crack climbing in the 5.9-to-5.11 range, with several ultra-classic (think Yosemite Valley here) 5.10 moderates. The 350-foot tall West Face, while shorter, is still exposed and dramatic and offers fabulous crack and chimney climbing in the 5.5-to-5.11 range. This face holds the mountain's Standard Route (5.5), which was the first route to the summit and is still considered an enjoyable undertaking today. The third major face is the Northeast Face. This face has far fewer routes and sees much less traffic than the other faces. As with any north-facing wall in the Selkirks, lichen coverage may play a challenging role when trying to climb it.

Chimney Rock, while very wild in character, sits in close proximity to two major trailheads. Both trailheads provide relatively straightforward approaches through excessively beautiful high country. Local climbers will chat endlessly about which approach is "better" or more "efficient" or perhaps even "more scenic." In reality, each approach offers its own unique sense of arrival to the dramatic faces of Chimney Rock, and both hold aesthetic value that are far beyond mere word descriptions in a guidebook. For the visiting rock climber, the chosen approach will probably have more to do with where you are driving from, rather than which one you may or may not prefer. The East Side Approach, via Upper Pack River Road, is a shorter drive from the Sandpoint/Missoula area, but the hike is longer and much steeper. The West Side Approach offers a shorter, but rougher, drive for those coming from the Spokane/Seattle area and a much shorter hike with much less elevation gain. In the end, both approaches offer great day-trip climbing opportunities at Chimney Rock and in the surrounding area.

As with any mountaineering challenge, it is best to get an early start if planning to climb Chimney Rock. Camping at or near the trailheads is a very wise choice for Chimney Rock visitors. If there are any thunderclouds in the vicinity of the Selkirk Crest, chances are they will be drawn into Chimney Rock like moths to a bug light. In fact, a half-century of human interactions with Chimney Rock has led to its local nickname of "Lightning Rod of the Selkirks." Plan accordingly.

Given the fact that Chimney Rock sits directly on the Selkirk Crest, its climbing season can be relatively short. Snow-covered approaches into July are not uncommon. And patches of snow often linger in the basin north of Mount Roothaan through August. During low snow years, however, it is possible to drive to both the Pack River and Mount Roothaan trailheads by Memorial Day weekend. During Indian summers, climbs of Chimney Rock have been reported through late October. In general, however, expect the climbing season to be from mid-June through late September.

The high-quality, granite rock climbing on Chimney Rock is generally characterized by splitter crack systems that offer incredible hand-jamming and strenuous liebacking situations high above the valley floor. Off-width cracks are a very common part of the Chimney Rock climbing experience. In fact, it is quite common for first-time visitors to underestimate the character of Chimney Rock and find themselves halfway up a pitch with only a tiny selection of TCUs left on their rack and 50 feet of off-hands 5.10 climbing left to surmount before the belay ledge. Some climbers may also find the grades to be a hair on the sandbag side. But please, don't let this stop you from climbing here. It makes the taste of victory that much sweeter. All in all, Chimney Rock has left few climbers disappointed in terms of wilderness scenery, rock quality and the overall feeling that simply clinging to these aesthetic walls is an incredible way to spend one's day. To paraphrase a famous Teddy Roosevelt quip, Chimney Rock climbers should "climb fast and carry a big rack."

History

According to Randall Green, in "Idaho Rock," the most legendary tale of climbing on Chimney Rock stems from the mountain's second recorded ascent, which occurred in 1935, one year after the mountain's first recorded ascent. John Boothe, whose parents owned a cabin on the shores of Priest Lake (roughly eight miles as the crow flies from Chimney Rock), decided one summer day that he would like to perform a round-trip climb of the peak from the cabin. Approaching via the south fork of Indian Creek, Boothe covered miles of roadless wild country, all alone, while dead-reckoning in the general direction of the peak. Once beneath it, he soloed the Standard Route (5.5), and then cruised back down to his cabin on the lake before sundown. This rather alarming feat would still be considered a major event even by today's high rock climbing standards.

The first ascent of the peak was completed by a team from the Seattle area made up of John Carey, Mart Chamberlain, Fred Theime and Bryon Ward via the West Face in 1934. This crew had undoubtedly honed their skills over in the renowned Cascade Range and implemented these skills to get to the summit of Chimney Rock. The party's ascent resulted in the establishment of the Standard Route (5.5), which is still considered a classic route today. The pioneering Seattle team successfully met its many challenges, a notable feat for their day.

Juli Russell on the Rappel Chimney route

For the next 30 years, the prized aspect of the mountain – the daunting East Face – was left unclimbed. It wasn't until August 1961 that Ed Cooper and Dave Hiser showed up and plucked the most obvious line directly up the center of the face. Cooper-Hiser (5.9) follows a series of cracks and lieback flakes and remains an area classic. The route was originally climbed using points of aid and was not free climbed until 1972, when John Roskelley and Chris Kopczynski of Spokane completed it.

The South Prow of Chimney Rock holds its own piece of climbing history. In 1968, the inexhaustible Fred Beckey appeared on the scene and plucked the line, which is by far the mountain's most striking geologic feature. Beckey, a renowned climber and author of several climbing and geology tomes on the Cascade Range, is the father of thousands of first ascents around the world. His presence on Chimney Rock – while not surprising – is a tangible tribute to the dramatic nature and quality of Chimney Rock, and it adds a flavorful footnote to the history of rock climbing here.

New route activity on Chimney Rock continued to blossom well into the 1970s and 1980s when groups of strong, motivated climbers from Sandpoint and Spokane began climbing some of the impossible-looking crack systems on the West and East Faces. Armed with hexentrics, rudimentary Friends and Swami belts, climbers such as John Roskelley, Chris Kopczynski, Dane Burns, Ron Burgner, Randall Green, Martin McBirney and many others, pioneered routes that, for their time, were miraculous displays of strength and crack-climbing skill.

In the 2000s, new route activity has slowed due to the fact that most of the major, obvious crack systems have been climbed. However, variations to older routes seem to be popping up here and there. It is certain that many of the newer routes and route variations – especially on the mountain's less-frequented North Face – have either not been recorded or were recorded in the historical summit register, which sat at the summit for years and was removed in 2004. It is only hoped that the caretakers of this historical artifact will ensure that this information is not lost forever. The routes that are included in this guidebook are the "tried and true" routes of Chimney Rock. It is hoped that further information on the variations and new routes on Chimney Rock will be relayed in further editions of this guidebook.

A Note on Climbing Gear

Due to Chimney Rock's varying-sized cracks, climbers should expect to carry a large rack containing a full set of stoppers and a full set of cams to 4 inches. Please note, however, that a majority of the routes on the East Face will require double sizes from 0.75 inch to 3 inches. Think Indian Creek here. Large hexes can be substituted at belay anchors where necessary.

A Note on Ethics

In recent years, Chimney Rock has been at the heart of an ethical debate concerning bolted belay and rappel anchors. It may have all begun in the summer of 2001 when Paul Haraf and I replaced existing bolts and removed old, manky belay slings in the Rappel Chimney, which has been the standard rappel route since 1935. With hardware donated by the American Safe Climbing Association, Paul and I hand-drilled four new, stainless steel, double-ring rappel bolts. The result of this effort was a much safer descent down the peak's standard descent route. The following summer, however, a new bolted rappel route was found on Cooper-Hiser, a route that has historically been a trad route with mostly gear anchors. It is understandable that people are constantly looking for a safer and more enjoyable climbing experience. However, sad is the day when suddenly all historic gear belay spots are peppered with bolts, or worse yet, bolts are used as means of protection, where decades of ascents required no such protection. We, the climbers, are our own land stewards out here. Chimney Rock is not federally protected under the 1964 Wilderness Act; indeed, it is not located within a designated Wilderness Area. Therefore bolting is technically legal. But this is not an excuse to do so. Please remember that Chimney Rock is wild in character, and only we can prevent further unnecessary bolting on this beautiful chunk of rock.

Camping

While trailhead car camping is the most common method of overnighting in the area, parties with multiday itineraries will find excellent backcountry camping within easy access of the peak. On the west side of Chimney Rock, a fairyland of subalpine meadows is located down below the talus basin just north of Mount Roothaan. To get there, follow the West Side Approach to the peak. Once you have gained the Mount Roothaan ridge crest, drop down into the broad basin north of the peak. Once you reach boulder fields at the bottom of the basin, hike down-valley in a northerly manner. Open stretches of meadow and rock slabs are located below the basin. Water is available here through late summer. In spring, or even early summer, when remnants of a snowpack are still lingering on the Mount Roothaan ridge crest, it is possible to camp here, utilizing the snow for meltwater. In high summer, however, no water is available on the ridge. On a side note, Priest Lake, which is passed while driving in via the West Side Approach, has various campgrounds on its eastern shore.

On the east side of Chimney Rock, nice camping meadows are located down among the trees below the peak's East Face. However, running water is generally not available here in late summer. Chimney Creek, which is encountered on the East Side approach, may be the closest water source to high camps on this side.

Amenities

If following the East Side approach via Upper Pack River Road, the café inside the gas station at the intersection of Highway 95 and Upper Pack River Road (roughly 20 miles from the Chimney Rock trailhead) offers some of the best home-cooked meals in the area. Breakfast burritos are taken to a whole new level here. Gas, pop, beer, ice, canned goods and other items can also be purchased. A pay phone and patron restrooms are also available.

If following the West Side Approach via Priest Lake, there is a café/store in the township of Coolin that offers excellent shakes, burgers, a small assortment of groceries and canned goods, pop and other beverages. Beer can be purchased for take-away at the neighboring bar. For those with extra time and a need for a real meal, drive around to the west side of Priest Lake and follow Highway 57 north to the town of Nordman.

Emergency Facilities

If following the East Side Approach via the Pack River Road, the gas station at the intersection of Highway 95 and the Pack River Road (roughly 20 miles from the Chimney Rock trailhead) offers the closest public pay phones. Sandpoint, Idaho, roughly 13 miles south of the gas station, offers the closest emergency facilities.

If following the West Side Approach via Priest Lake, the township of Coolin (roughly 18 miles from the Mount Roothaan trailhead) offers the closest public pay phone. However, Newport, Washington, roughly 36 miles southwest of Coolin on Highway 2, offers the closest emergency facilities.

West Side Approach

Getting There

Take Highway 57 north from Priest River, Idaho, approximately 23 miles and turn right (east) toward the township of Coolin. Go about 5.25 miles to Coolin and turn right (east) onto Cavanaugh Bay Road. Travel another three miles or so and veer right on East Shore Road, following this about 4.5 miles to Road No. 24 (Hunt Creek Road), which is located a few yards past a cement bridge spanning Hunt Creek. Turn onto Road 24 (a dirt road) and follow it for four miles to its junction with Road 2. Bear left and go 1.6 miles to Road 25. Keep straight for about a mile to a fork, bear right, then go 0.3 miles to another fork and bear left. Proceed up Road 25 for four miles via a rough road that may require high-clearance vehicles. After a major right-hand switchback, the road gets even rougher. Some parties may elect to park at this final switchback and proceed the last 0.5 miles to the trailhead on foot. The road dead-ends at the Mount Roothaan trailhead, where an old fire lookout once sat. A large parking area here will accommodate many vehicles and provides excellent car camping opportunities. A pit toilet is located in the trees on the north side of the parking area. Please note that Chimney Rock cannot be seen on this drive in. Mount Roothaan and Gunsight Peak block any such views. It only becomes visible after you crest the Mount Roothaan shoulder during the hike in.

Approach

From the Mount Roothaan trailhead, pick up a good trail on the east side of the parking area that winds through thick timber. After roughly 1.5 miles, the trail comes to a series of steep, sandy switchbacks that climb up to a broad ridge crest on Mount Roothaan. The true summit of Mount Roothaan lies to the south. From this vantage point, you get your first views of Chimney Rock and its aesthetic West Face.

Two options exist at this point. If you are headed for climbs on the West Face, it is possible to drop directly into the basin on the north side of Mount Roothaan via a climber's trail. Once in the basin, hike overland in the general direction of Chimney Rock, staying near the base of the steep wall (the Roothaan Cirque) that is on your right (east) side. A series of climber's trails on grassy benches beneath this wall leads to the base of Chimney Rock's West Face.

Alternatively, drop off the north side of Mount Roothaan but stay high and curve east, following climbers' trails and cairns, until you gain a pass just east of the summit of Mount Roothaan. Continue scrambling along rock benches near the crest of the Roothaan Cirque, staying on its west side. Gain a notch in the skyline, which is easily seen from the Mount Roothaan ridge on the hike in. Down-climb off the east side of the notch and continue in a northeasterly manner toward the East Face of Chimney Rock. The total hiking distance is roughly 3.5 miles and should take anywhere from 1.5 to 2 hours.

(Author's Note: A climber's trail located on the north side of Chimney Rock links the East and West Faces).

East Side Approach

Getting There

From Sandpoint, Idaho, drive north on Highway 95 for 13 miles and turn left (west) onto Road No. 231 (Upper Pack River Road).* Go about 16 miles to West Branch Road No. 2653, turn left and go one-half mile to the Chimney Rock Trail No. 256 trailhead.

*The Pack River Bridge located 11 miles from the highway washed out in 2006 and will be closed through the 2007 climbing season. Climbers may access the trailhead by any means other than highway vehicles, including mountain bike or ATVs.

Approach

From the trailhead, follow an old logging road for a couple of miles until it turns into trail near Chimney Creek. Climb up through steep, timbered terrain to a ridge with granite benches and good views of Chimney Rock. Continue higher, entering a broad basin below the East Face, and hike up to the base of your route of choice. This approach is roughly six miles long and should take between 2.5 to 3.5 hours.

A Note on Descents

From the summit of Chimney Rock, rappelling is the only option for descent. The historical and most commonly used descent is via the "rappel chimney" located on the northwest edge of the summit area. One short, single-rope rappel from the summit brings you to the West Face belay "notch." A second single-rope rappel brings you to relatively new, double-ring anchors on a rock pillar inside the rappel chimney. A third single-rope rappel from here puts you on the sandy ledge below West Face Girls. From here, down-climbing is needed to gain the base of the West Face. To avoid this short but exposed down-climb, use the fixed anchors on the Sancho's belay ledge as a fourth single-rope rappel option.

A rappel route down the East Face is made possible by scrambling down ledges on the southeast tip of the summit area to chain anchors located directly above the South Nose Exit. A single-rope rappel (60 feet) brings you to a second pair of chain anchors on blocks above Magnum Force. From here, a double-rope rappel (120 feet) takes you to Prow Ledge at the base of Magnum Force. A third double-rope rappel (140 feet) from Prow Ledge gets you to the base of the East Face.

Please remember that the only way to hike between the West and East Faces is via a climber's trail located on the north side of Chimney Rock. No circumnavigation of the peak via foot is possible.

Belay/
Rappel
"Notch"

South
Nose

CHIMNEY ROCK WEST FACE
SA) Sancho's (II 5.9)
SD) Sancho's Direct (II 5.10b R)
TC) Twin Cracks (5.10a)
WG) West Side Girls (5.10a R)
RC) Rappel Chimney (II 5.7)
SR) Standard Route (I+ 5.5)
WD) West Face Direct (II 5.9-)
WI) Wish He Were She (II 5.10d R)

SF) Sticky Fingers (II 5.10d R)
SU) Scuffin-Up (II 5.9)
IH) It Ain't Hay (II 5.9)
BB) Berg's Breeze (II 5.10c R)
BC) Black Cat (II 5.11c)
FR) Fun Roof (5.10b)
AT) Air Time (5.10b R)
YR) Youranalysis (5.11b)
SN) South Nose Exit (5.9+)

West Face

SA) Sancho's (5.9) 3 pitches/gear to 4 inches

This climb is a great lesson in off-width climbing technique. Sancho's follows an obvious crack line up the far left (north) edge of the West Face. Some lichen does exist on this route and may increase the challenges of climbing it.

Pitch 1: Begin by climbing flakes and cracks located below and to the left of West Side Girls – the obvious open book formation described later in this section. Climb discontinuous cracks to a short right-facing corner. This corner leads to a broad ledge with a fixed anchor on its far right side.

Pitch 2: On the left side of the broad ledge, climb the obvious, right-facing corner/crack system. Tricky liebacking and stemming follows this right-trending wide crack directly to the West Face belay "notch" (gear to 4 inches).

Pitch 3: From the "notch," move around left to easier terrain and climb up through blocks to the top. Belay from double-ring rap anchors a few yards shy of the summit. (Note: These anchors mark the standard "rappel chimney" descent route.)

SD) Sancho's Direct (5.10b R) 2 pitches/gear to 3.5 inches

This rarely traveled route begins just right of the second pitch of Sancho's on the broad ledge system. The route is characterized by a thin, hard-to-protect crack followed by runout face climbing.

Pitch 1: Start on the belay ledge just right of the Sancho's corner/crack system. Climb delicately up a thin crack, which leads to a runout face directly above. Stay out right of the Sancho's crack system via face climbing, rejoining the crack just below the West Face "notch."

Pitch 2: From the "notch," move around left to easier terrain and climb up through blocks to the top. Belay from double-ring rap anchors a few yards shy of the summit. (Note: These anchors mark the standard "rappel chimney" descent route.)

TC) Twin Cracks (5.10a) 1 pitch/gear to 3 inches

This one-pitch route climbs the double cracks on the inside left wall of the open book formation called West Side Girls. Begin by scrambling up fourth-class rock steps to a sandy belay ledge directly below the open book. Climb the double cracks and belay off fixed anchors on the Sancho's ledge system.

WG) West Side Girls (5.10a R) 1 pitch/gear to 1 inch

A classic open-book formation that is very thin and very difficult to protect. Scramble up fourth-class rock steps directly below the open book to a sandy ledge. Climb directly up the open book, and belay off the Sancho's fixed anchor. This route is frequently top roped on the way down the "rappel chimney" descent route.

RC) Rappel Chimney (5.7) 4 pitches/gear to 2 inches

The second-easiest route to the summit of Chimney Rock, this route only briefly climbs the actual "rappel chimney" that is rappelled down during the standard

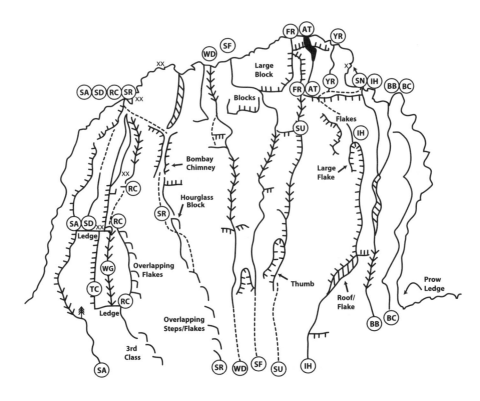

CHIMNEY ROCK WEST FACE
SA) Sancho's (II 5.9)
SD) Sancho's Direct (II 5.10b R)
TC) Twin Cracks (5.10a)
WG) West Side Girls (5.10a R)
RC) Rappel Chimney (II 5.7)

SR) Standard Route (I+ 5.5)
WD) West Face Direct (II 5.9-)
SF) Sticky Fingers (II 5.10d R)
SU) Scuffin-Up (II 5.9
FR) Fun Roof (5.10b)
AT) Air Time (5.10b R)

YR) Youranalysis (5.11b)
IH) It Ain't Hay (II 5.9)
BB) Berg's Breeze (II 5.10c R)
BC) Black Cat (II 5.11c)
SN) South Nose Exit (5.9+)

descent off Chimney Rock. In reality, it climbs a fairly serpentine route that starts down and right of the chimney system, crosses it at half-height and ends via a corner system to climber's right of the second belay.

Pitch 1: Begin by scrambling up fourth-class steps that lead to the ledge system below West Side Girls. Just shy of the ledge, begin traversing up and right on ledges and overlaps following the path of least resistance. The goal is to climb until even with the Sancho's belay ledge and then traverse directly left to the anchors.

Pitch 2: From the belay ledge, climb directly up the chimney proper to a small roof/bulge. A stout move up and over the right side of the bulge brings you to the base of a rock pillar with new (replaced in 2001) double-ring rappel anchors.

Pitch 3: From the anchors, step directly out right about 20 feet (leaving the chimney system) and locate a corner system with green lichen on its inside walls. Climb the corner via fun hand jams and excellent exposure over the land.

At the top of the corner, move left and scramble up to the "notch" and belay.

Pitch 4: From the "notch," move around left to easier terrain and climb up through blocks to the top. Belay from double-ring rap anchors a few yards shy of the summit. (Note: These anchors mark the standard "rappel chimney" descent route.)

SR) Standard Route (5.5) 3 pitches/gear to 3 inches

Originally rated 5.3, this is the easiest route to the summit. Route finding can be problematic on this route. It is best to remember that the route climbs a diagonal line starting just left of center on the West Face and finishes at the belay "notch" in the upper horizon. The main feature on the route is a wide Bombay chimney on the second pitch that offers excellent hand cracks, good pro and lots of exposure. This is a truly classic mountain ramble.

Pitch 1: Begin on easy, overlapping granite steps just left of center on the West Face. Climb diagonally up and left via steps and short corners to a large hourglass-shaped belay block perched on a ledge (some slings may exist on the block).

Pitch 2: From the belay block, look up and left and notice the open, flaring Bombay chimney slot. Climb up a ramp, aiming for the chimney slot. Stem and jam the Bombay chimney, watching for loose flakes and soaking in the exposure. Once above the Bombay chimney, move directly left via ledges and slabs and gain the West Face belay "notch."

Pitch 3: From the "notch," move around left to easier terrain and climb up through blocks to the top. Belay from double-ring rap anchors a few yards shy of the summit. (Note: These anchors mark the standard "rappel chimney" descent route.)

WD) West Face Direct (5.9-) 3 pitches/gear to 4 to 5 inches

In the center of the West Face, just right of the Standard Route, locate an obvious corner system about a third of the way up the face. This is the major corner system of West Face Direct.

Pitch 1: Scramble up fourth-/fifth-class steps to the base of the corner and belay.

Pitch 2: Climb the off-width corner direct (gear to 5 inches). Partway up the pitch, look for a small crack on the left wall to use for pro. Belay from a ledge above the corner.

Pitch 3: Move up past a dead tree and climb cracks and blocks to the next major flake system on the left. Climb flakes and cracks to the top.

WI) Wish He Were She (5.10d R) 2 pitches/gear to 3 inches

This route follows the obvious, thin crack between West Face Direct and Sticky Fingers and joins the latter just below summit blocks (shown on page 98).

Pitch 1: Scramble up fourth-class on left side of large, detached flake, which sits in the center of the lower face and belay at the base of the West Face Direct corner.

Pitch 2: Swing right, jam and lieback the thin crack straight up to the loose rubble ledge where route joins Sticky Fingers. Can be done in one long pitch to summit or belay from rubble ledge and finish with short pitch through summit blocks.

SF) Sticky Fingers (5.10d R) 3 pitches/gear to 3 inches plus micro cams/nuts

This route is characterized by a thin, zigzagging crack that cuts through a patch of yellow lichen just right of the wide corner system on West Face Direct.

Pitch 1: Climb the right or left side of a large, detached flake that sits in the center of the lower face. Follow a thin (finger tip) crack system above, passing through the zigzag crack and belay on a ledge out right.

Pitch 2: A strenuous, thin crack system (hard to protect) marks the next portion of the climb. Once confronted by a large block above, bear left to easier terrain. Some loose rocks on a ledge system mark the belay.

Pitch 3: Follow the line of least resistance up through blocks and some loose sections to the top. Alternatively, it is possible to traverse directly right and gain ledges that eventually lead to the South Nose Exit.

SU) Scuffin-Up (5.9) 3 pitches/gear to 3 inches

Scuffin-Up is a free version of an old aid line called Broken Thumb. A large, detached flake the shape of a thumb marks the beginning of the route. The "thumb" is located just right of center on the West Face and is most easily seen while standing directly beneath it. It is possible to start out right of the thumb and gain the corner system above it. Some route-finding skills must be employed to avoid off-width cracks.

Pitch 1: Journey up the right side of the thumb via the path of least resistance, stepping into the main crack system directly above it. Continue up the corner via liebacking and jamming. It is possible to belay from slings inside the corner system prior to the flaring, wide slot above.

Pitch 2: "Scuff up" the flaring slot, pulling into a brief corner system, followed by more cracks that lead to a spacious ledge system below a massive roof.

Pitch 3: Finish via Fun Roof, Air Time, Youranalysis or by traversing out right to the South Nose Exit.

IH) It Ain't Hay (5.9) 2 pitches/gear to 3 inches

This excellent climb is often referred to as the "best route on the West Face" and is characterized by a prominent, right-slanting roof/flake system on the first pitch. It is a great warm-up for harder routes on the East Face.

Pitch 1: Climb discontinuous cracks below the left edge of the right-trending roof/flake system. Traverse out right directly beneath the roof/flake system (or by under-clinging the actual roof/flake) to a short, steep wall with a hand crack. Jam and lieback directly up the crack to a stance. Continue up the remainder of the crack that leads to a large, detached flake. Chimney up behind the flake to its top and belay on a pedestal.

Pitch 2: Locate a curving flake running out left of the belay pedestal. The initial portion of the flake is a steep right-facing, lieback problem followed by an excellent, left-trending hand traverse. Traverse out left until the flake steepens and thins. Here, step directly out left onto a ledge and traverse roughly 20 feet farther left. Pull up over onto another ledge and traverse directly out right to the South Nose. This is a somewhat wandering but excellent pitch.

Pitch 3: Finish via Fun Roof, Air Time, Youranalysis, or by traversing out right to the South Nose Exit.

BB) Berg's Breeze (5.10c R) 2 pitches/gear to 4 inches

On the far right edge of the West Face, locate a shallow open book with a thin crack at its back that leads to an off-width section above.

Pitch 1: Stem the initial corner system, pulling into the off-width section via swearing. Thrash up the off-width section for several feet. Avoid the upper, ugly, wide slot with loose blocks by stepping left into an alcove with slings. Belay here.

Pitch 2: From the alcove, pull through the steep roof above via hand cracks and some runout face moves. Belay on the skyline below the South Nose and finish via the South Nose Exit.

BC) Black Cat (5.11c) 1 pitch/gear to 3 inches with extra fingertip-sized stuff

The arching crack system to the right of Berg's Breeze is It Ain't Hay on steroids: strenuous, fingertip liebacking to a hand-crack finish. Begin in the obvious crack system and perform a single, lengthy pitch all the way to the ledge below the South Nose Exit.

Note: The next four wild adventures offer direct pitches to the summit of Chimney Rock after climbing Scuffin-Up, It Ain't Hay or Sticky Fingers.

FR) Fun Roof (5.10b) 1 pitch/gear to 4 inches

Access this strenuous, exposed roof from the broad ledge system above Scuffin-Up and It Ain't Hay. Climb the corner system below the large roof above the far left side of the ledge. Jam, under-cling and smear out the large, ominous roof, gaining an unexpected but good hand jam crack that leads to the summit. This climb can be very scary to second if the leader does not protect it well.

AT) Air Time (5.10b R) 1 pitch/gear to 4 inches

From the broad ledge system above Scuffin-Up and It Ain't Hay, review the ominous roof above. The center of the roof is split by a flaring Bombay chimney that looks, and is, quite difficult to protect. Climb up through this off-width crack and flounder to the top.

YR) Youranalysis (5.11b) 1 pitch/gear to 2 inches

From the broad ledge system above Scuffin-Up and It Ain't Hay, locate a small dihedral on the right side of the roof system that rises through the roof via a thin finger crack. Climb this finger crack to the summit.

SN) South Nose Exit (5.9+) 1 pitch/1 bolt plus gear to 1.5 inches

The South Nose of Chimney Rock is a truly exposed (and oftentimes gusty) prow of rock that marks the convergence of the West and East Faces. Several routes on both faces lead to the South Nose Exit, which is used as means of reaching the summit area. The South Nose is characterized by a steep, rectangular face covered with patches of yellow lichen. A single bolt protects the face. Adequate gear is found higher up. Start at the base of the steep wall directly in the middle of the face and below the bolt. Climb up to the bolt and then traverse out left, palming the very crest of the nose at times (nice exposure here) followed by a brief mantle move that ends at a broad ledge a few feet below the summit.

South Nose Exit →

CHIMNEY ROCK EAST FACE
LG) Lord Greystoke (5.11b)
UN) UNI (5.11+)
MF) Magnum Force (II 5.10b)
WL) White Lightning (5.11d)
SI) Sudden Impact (II 5.11b)
WS) Wayward Son (II 5.10a)

KI) Kimmie (II 5.11c)
YA) Yahoody (II 5.11b)
EF) East Face Direct (II 5.10b)
CL) Canary Legs (5.10b)
CH) Cooper–Hiser (II 5.9)
V) Direct Finish Variation (5.9)
TS) Tsunami (II+ 5.11d R)

IS) Illusions (5.11a)
FF) Free Friends (II+ 5.10c)
ET) Eye of the Tiger (II 5.11a)
NE) Northeast Face (II 5.10d R)
GM) Graymatter (II 5.11c)

East Face

LG) Lord Greystoke (5.11b) 1 pitch/gear to 2 inches

This route begins on a ledge-system partway up the left side of the East Face but below the South Prow of Chimney Rock. To gain this ledge (Prow Ledge), either climb Sudden Impact or Wayward Son, or hike around to the West Face and gain the ledge by curving around the far right (south) edge of the face below the South Prow. Lord Greystoke climbs the gently overhanging finger and thin-hands crack on the far left (west) side of Prow Ledge. Strenuous moves lead to a 5.10 mantle move below chain anchors. Lower off.

UN) UNI (5.11+) 1 pitch/gear to 1.5 inches

This is the thin crack just right of Lord Greystoke. Above the thin crack, climb the obvious, leaning dihedral to the top of Magnum Force.

MF) Magnum Force (5.10b) 2 pitches/1 bolt plus gear to 4 inches

Twenty feet to the right of Lord Greystoke, locate a steep, white granite wall split by a beautiful lieback flake that runs directly above Prow Ledge (see the Lord Greystoke description for access to Prow Ledge).

Pitch 1: Follow the crack system until it widens (obvious off-width) at roughly half height. Bolts protect this very wide section. Continue up the crack to a rest behind a block, then move up left to easier terrain. The obvious belay nook above is historically referred to as "the window."

Pitch 2: Follow fifth-class terrain up slabs and ledges to the South Nose Exit, which is climbed to the summit.

WL) White Lightning (5.11d) 1 pitch/fixed piton, small TCUs, gear to 4.5 inches

The most striking and obvious crack system on the East Face, this crack splits the white rock to the right of Magnum Force. Climb directly above the fixed anchor belay on Prow Ledge, connecting thin crack systems to a sloping ledge where a 1.25-inch splitter crack goes straight up to the lightning bolts. The route joins Magnum Force at its signature off-width.

Rappel off or continue to top via South Nose Exit.

SI) Sudden Impact (5.11b) 1 pitch/fixed pitons plus gear to 2 inches

This climb begins at the base of the East Face and ends at Prow Ledge below Lord Greystoke and Magnum Force. Begin by climbing a hand crack that leads into a left-facing corner system. From a shelf above the left-facing corner, move up into a thin, right-facing corner that is protected by old pitons. Belay on Prow Ledge.

WS) Wayward Son (5.10a) 2 pitches/gear to 3 inches

A somewhat contrived and wandering route, Wayward Son climbs the first section of Kimmie, then moves left partway up the pitch, traverses below the upper corner system of Sudden Impact and finishes via an easier corner to the left of it.

Pitch 1: Begin by climbing up a ramp/flake system on the lower left side of the East Face that leads to a small tree. Continue up and left into Kimmie, a steep, finger-tip lieback crack that leads to a small ledge partway up.

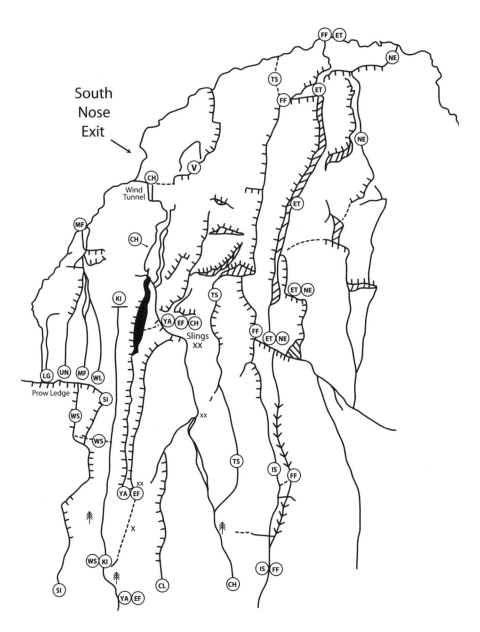

South Nose Exit

Wind Tunnel

Slings XX

Prow Ledge

CHIMNEY ROCK EAST FACE
LG) Lord Greystoke (5.11b)
UN) UNI (5.11+)
MF) Magnum Force (II 5.10b)
WL) White Lightning (5.11d)
SI) Sudden Impact (II 5.11b)

WS) Wayward Son (II 5.10a)
KI) Kimmie (II 5.11c)
YA) Yahoody (II 5.11b)
EF) East Face Direct (II 5.10b)
CL) Canary Legs (5.10b)
CH) Cooper-Hiser (II 5.9)

V) Direct Finish Variation (5.9)
TS) Tsunami (II+ 5.11d R)
IS) Illusions (5.11a)
FF) Free Friends (II+ 5.10c)
ET) Eye of the Tiger (II 5.11a)
NE) Northeast Face (II 5.10d R)

Pitch 2: From this ledge, traverse directly out left, stepping down at one point to gain the ledge system below the crux corner of Sudden Impact. Continue moving left to the next major corner, which is formed by a block leaning against the main wall. Climb this corner to Prow Ledge.

KI) Kimmie (5.11c) 1 pitch/gear to 2 inches

Begin by climbing the ramp/flake system on the lower left side of the East Face, which leads to a small tree. Continue up into a steep finger-tip, lieback crack that becomes increasingly thin and tricky. The crack eventually fades out and ends at a set of fixed anchors. Lower off.

YA) Yahoody (5.11b) 2 pitches/gear to 4 inches

A classic crack of varying size, this route is often referred to as the "best 5.11 at Chimney Rock." It is undoubtedly one of the most aesthetic.

Pitch 1: Begin by climbing up a ramp/flake system on the lower left side of the East Face, which leads to a small tree. Climb a tricky 5.10 face up and right past pinches and grooves that leads to a small belay stance signified by a two-bolt anchor.

Pitch 2: Step left, attacking the crack directly above, which passes through a couple of small roofs. A severely off-width section higher up forces you out right and across a sloping ledge to join the main belay station on Cooper-Hiser. Finish via Cooper-Hiser or rap off; use rappel points (double rings) located on Cooper-Hiser.

EF) East Face Direct (5.10b) 2 to 3 pitches/gear to 4 inches

This climb begins as for Yahoody but traverses right at the small belay stance above the tricky 5.10 face, finishing via the strenuous curving crack above.

Pitch 1: Begin by climbing up a ramp/flake system on the lower left side of the East Face, which leads to a small tree. Climb a tricky 5.10 face up and right past pinches and grooves that leads to a small belay stance signified by a two-bolt anchor.

Pitch 2: Move up and into the obvious, right-curving crack/flake system to the right of Yahoody which rises through a roof/bulge high above. Strenuous moves carry you up through the crack and through the bulge to a ledge, where it is possible to traverse up and right to the main belay station on top of the first pitch of Cooper-Hiser. Finish via Cooper-Hiser or rap off, utilizing rappel points (double rings) located on Cooper-Hiser.

(Note: It is possible to continue climbing past the Cooper-Hiser belay, joining the second pitch of Cooper-Hiser and ending on the ledge directly next to the Wind Tunnel – completing a 190-foot, incredible mega-pitch.)

CL) Canary Legs (5.10b) 1 pitch/gear to 4 inches

A great introduction to crack climbing at Chimney Rock, this excellent pitch can be used as an alternative to the first pitch of Cooper-Hiser, which can be intimidating for some climbers. Begin in the obvious splitter crack located just left of Cooper-Hiser's first pitch. Jam and lieback up the excellent crack for roughly 75 feet until a thin traverse forces you up and right. Belay from new, double-ring rap anchors located in the gully partway up the first pitch of Cooper-Hiser.

Left Variation: Just left of Canary Legs is another crack that makes up the left side of a large, detached flake. This crack is a variation of the original Canary Legs crack and is said to be 5.10b and very delightful.

CH) Cooper-Hiser (5.9) 3 pitches/gear to 3 inches

A classic moderate, Cooper-Hiser is the type of climb that never loses its ability to challenge and inspire even the most jaded trad climber. Most parties will elect to muscle up Canary Legs (5.10b) to avoid the first section of Cooper-Hiser's original first pitch.

Pitch 1: A fairly intimidating lead, this pitch travels up the obvious, left-trending crack system with a dead tree halfway up. Grovel up the crack past the tree (tricky pro), and enter a sandy gully system. A double-ring anchor on a rock pillar farther up the gully is often used as a belay. However, it is best to continue up the gully and into a series of cracks, finishing this long pitch on a sloping ledge with rappel rings, which is the main belay station for the climb. (Please note that new double-ring anchors may have replaced the old sling anchor at the main belay station before the time of publication.)

Pitch 2: From the main belay station, traverse directly out left, aiming for flakes and corners that rise into a series of lieback cracks higher up. Excellent jamming and liebacking leads up the gut of the face. Near the top, a thin lieback flake out left is a better option than the wide flake on your right. Step left into this beautiful flake and continue up to a short, off-width section that ends on a broad ledge beside the cavernous gash known as The Wind Tunnel.

Pitch 3: This pitch involves gaining the base of the South Nose Exit (5.9+) via a gaping maw of rock known as the Wind Tunnel. From the belay ledge, walk left and enter the tunnel. At a point where the tunnel narrows, it is possible to chimney up it using each wall for friction. The climbing is easy, but the pro is hard to find.

V) Direct Finish Variation (5.9) 1 pitch/Gear to 4 inches

From the top of the second pitch on Cooper-Hiser, climb the 4-inch lieback crack to the right of the belay anchors. Traverse directly right at the top of the crack and endure a frantic mantle move that leads to a ledge. Follow the line of least resistance to the top.

TS) Tsunami (5.11d R) 3 pitches/Gear to 4 inches

A tremendous, surfboard-shaped roof smack in the middle of the East Face offers a daunting obstacle when viewed from below. Tsunami punches directly up through this roof and connects with the final pitches of Free Friends.

Pitch 1: Begin by climbing the first pitch of Cooper-Hiser. Once past the dead tree, enter the sandy gully system for a handful of feet before stepping out right into a thin crack system. A hanging belay may be required here.

Pitch 2: Jam up toward the ominous roof, passing through a brief, off-width section before tackling the hand-crack that splits the center of the roof. Continue past the roof for several feet until you reach a ledge in the main crack system of Free Friends.

Pitch 3: Finish as for Free Friends, or, more daringly, climb the main crack sys-

Julie Dietrich on Free Friends

tem of Free Friends, but instead of continuing out right as for that climb's standard finish, climb the blank wall directly up and left to the summit. There is no pro on this face, and it is probably best top roped.

IS) Illusions (5.11a) 1 pitch/gear to 3 inches

The next major crack system to the right of Cooper-Hiser is characterized by twin cracks. The upper, left crack is a one-pitch route called Illusions, and the upper right crack is the first pitch of Free Friends. Begin by climbing a ramp system to the base of the cracks. Enter a beautiful, lieback finger crack and continue up the leftmost crack via devious fingertip holds. Higher up, the crack widens and eases back, finishing on a ledge shared with Free Friends. Finish via Free Friends or Eye of the Tiger.

FF) Free Friends (5.10c) 3 pitches/gear to 4 inches

A classic moderate that offers every possible type of crack climbing skill there is, Free Friends is a long-time, local favorite and a must-do for any 5.10 trad climber visiting the area. The route traverses under the large surfboard-shaped roof smack in the middle of the East Face, the same roof that Tsunami climbs directly up through.

Pitch 1: Begin by climbing as for Illusions via a ramp system to a ledge below the twin cracks. Climb the leftmost crack (Illusions) for a few feet to a small stance. Move right into a wide crack leading into a slightly overhanging hand crack that leads to a sloping ledge. Traverse directly left through exposed but easy moves to access a large belay platform directly below the surfboard-shaped roof.

Pitch 2: Climb the obvious lieback flake that rises to join the left side of the roof. Jam and under-cling out right underneath the roof, turning the roof on its far right edge. Enter a long, strenuous crack/flake system and climb it to a large ledge on the right just below the summit.

Pitch 3: Traverse out right over blocks and locate an exposed crack through a small roof directly above. Interesting moves lead through the roof directly onto the summit area. A truly rewarding and excellent rock climb, this is one of the best multi-pitch 5.10 trad routes in the Pacific Northwest.

ET) Eye of the Tiger (5.11a) 3 pitches/gear to 4 inches

This climb starts on the belay ledge located on the top of the first pitch of Free Friends or Illusions. Directly above the ledge is a crack that leads to a second, higher ledge, which sits at the base of a massive, obvious right-facing corner system that is created by a protruding flake/pinnacle on climber's left. Eye of the Tiger climbs a direct route up the right-facing corner/crack system via strenuous and insecure fist jams.

Pitch 1: From the ledge above the first pitch of Free Friends or Illusions, climb cracks to the top of a block to a ledge historically referred to as the Micro-Scuzzem.

Pitch 2: Climb the steep, right-facing corner above to an awkward flare. Continue up and over a strenuous bulge and into a fist-sized (3-inch parallel sided) crack. Several 3-inch to 3.5-inch pieces are useful here. Belay at the top of the huge flake/pinnacle.

Pitch 3: Finish via the last pitch of Free Friends or by traversing up and right on easy ledges to the summit.

NE) Northeast Face (5.10d R) 3 pitches/gear to 3 inches

This climb also starts on the belay ledge at the top of the first pitch of Free Friends or Illusions.

Pitch 1: This pitch is the same as for Eye of the Tiger. From the ledge above the first pitch of Free Friends or Illusions, climb cracks to the top of a block to a ledge historically referred to as the Micro-Scuzzem.

Pitch 2: Face climb directly out right from the belay onto the main Northeast Face. Follow broken, discontinuous cracks to a ledge just right of the main flake/pinnacle.

Pitch 3: Move out right via easy ledges to the summit.

GM) Graymatter (5.11c) 3 pitches/gear to 3 inches

On the far right side of the Northeast Face, locate a relatively clean, gray corner system capped by a small roof. This is the crux corner of Graymatter, which is not very popular, yet considered the best route on this somewhat dirty and ominous face.

Pitch 1: Begin in a grungy crack that leads to awkward moves around a small roof. Pass bushes and a huge, loose block, and belay on a ledge at the base of the large, gray dihedral.

Pitch 2: Pass a large, loose block with caution and enter the main, gray-colored corner system. Climb toward the roof (several 2-inch pieces helpful) via a dihedral, passing the roof on its right. Easier slabs above lead to a belay alcove on the left.

Pitch 3: Climb a hand crack on the left that goes directly up to ledges and the summit.

Stained Window (5.10) (Not Shown) 2 pitches (long)/gear to 3.5 inches

This route shares the start with Graymatter but heads up left into easier ground.

Pitch 1: Same as for Graymatter, but diverge left about mid-height of first pitch and continue up hand cracks past a small roof to a small ledge.

Pitch 2: From the ledge, climb up and right, wandering left when possible to avoid difficulties. Near the summit blocks, work up and right to easier ground.

Honorable Mention: The Roothaan Cirque

While hiking into Chimney Rock (especially via the West Side Approach), it is hard to ignore the tall, looming rock walls that stretch northeast from Mount Roothaan to Chimney Rock. Numerous routes have been climbed on these rock faces, which is known collectively as the Roothaan Cirque. While many ascents have undoubtedly been lost to the years, a handful of routes remain as viable options to the climbs on nearby Chimney Rock.

North Nose (5.8) (Not Shown) 1 pitch/gear to 3 inches

The north ridge of the Roothaan Cirque terminates at a notch that separates Chimney Rock from the rest of the cirque. Near the tip of this ridge (on its northwest side) is a line that ascends through flakes and blocks to the top. Start this one-pitch climb by scrambling up slabs to the base of the steeper climbing. Follow discontinuous flakes and cracks through blocks to the top.

Notchos (5.8) (Not Shown) 2 pitches/gear to 3 inches

This climb begins on the east side of the notch between the Roothaan Cirque and Chimney Rock, about 50 yards left of Sudden Impact.

Pitch 1: Ascend a right-slanting flake system that ends at a prominent ledge directly below the notch.

Pitch 2: Follow a flake system directly up. Strenuous liebacking leads up through a series of ledges to the notch.

Black Crack (5.8) (Not Shown) 2 pitches/gear to 3 inches

This climb follows flakes and ledge systems on the left side of the notch (East Face) to an obvious, black crack, which is followed to the top.

Pitch 1: Climb a flake to a long, narrow ledge. Move right and face climb to a larger flake that is detached from the main face. Once past this wide flake, climb easier ground past a dead tree and then up to a live tree and belay.

Pitch 2: A diamond-shaped block must be passed to gain the upper black crack. Jam and lieback the black crack to the top of the notch.

Descent: Walk southwest along the Roothaan Cirque crest until it is possible to scramble down to a low point on the crest. Scramble south down to the base of the wall. Hike back east toward the base of the East Face of Chimney Rock.

Silver Dollar Peak ━ ━ ━ ━ ━ ━ ━ ━ ━ ━ ━

Silver Dollar Peak, (7,181 feet)

Number of Routes: One

Grade: 5.4

Length: Approximately 4 pitches

Approach Time: 3 to 4 hours

Climbing Time: 2 to 4 hours

Total Elevation Gain (car to summit): 3,161 feet (via the East Approach), 1,090 feet (via the West Approach)

Descent Type: Walk-off

Season: Generally June through late September

Maps: USGS The Wigwams (7.5-minute series) or USGS Bonners Ferry (1:100,000-scale metric)

Silver Dollar Peak is an aesthetic, pyramid-shaped wedge of granite located roughly two miles northeast of Chimney Rock on the Selkirk Crest. When viewed from the east, especially from Highway 95 just north of Sandpoint, Silver Dollar Peak appears as a small, pointy dot on the horizon. It is a member of the Seven Sisters group, which defines the Selkirk skyline. When seen from the southwest, especially from Chimney Rock, Silver Dollar Peak appears as a sheer slice of rock with a sharp west ridge formed by the forces of glacial rub and weathering.

Considered by some to be a classic mountaineering route, the West Ridge of Silver Dollar Peak cannot be compared to the nearby routes of Chimney Rock in terms of quality or challenge. However, the West Ridge of Silver Dollar is a fun, interesting mountain ramble, especially in terms of exposure, remoteness and its position high above the North Fork of Indian Creek. Some parties may elect to climb Silver Dollar Peak in conjunction with a weekend spent in the Chimney Rock area, or as a long day trip from either the Chimney Rock Trail No. 256 trailhead or the Mount Roothaan trailhead. Additionally, parties who are looking to hike a long, point-to-point stretch of the Selkirk Crest may wish to pack a small rack and a short rope and bag this ridge in conjunction with a multiday outing.

Getting There

As with Chimney Rock, both the Mount Roothaan trailhead (accessed via Priest Lake) and the Chimney Rock trailhead (accessed via Upper Pack River Road) offer access to Silver Dollar Peak. Depending on which way you are driving from (i.e. via Sandpoint, Idaho, or Spokane, Washington) follow the driving and hiking directions in the Chimney Rock section on pages 96-97. Please note that hiking into Silver Dollar Peak begins by first hiking into Chimney Rock and then continuing north along the Selkirk Crest.

SILVER DOLLAR PEAK
A) Approach (via Chimney Rock)
D) Descent (Walk-Off)

Approach (from Chimney Rock)

From Chimney Rock, follow the Selkirk Crest in a northeasterly manner (overland, brushy travel). Keep to the crest for easiest travel. After roughly 1.5 miles, you gain a small saddle on the Selkirk Crest just south of Silver Dollar Peak's summit where you can see, in profile, the mountain's West Ridge. The climbing route follows the left skyline if looking directly at the peak. From the saddle, hike off its west side and begin contouring under the West Face of Silver Dollar Peak, aiming for an obvious gendarme on the West Ridge. Once directly below the gendarme, follow gullies up and to the right (east) of it and gain a notch on the ridge crest between the gendarme and the summit. Rope up here.

West Ridge (5.4) 4 to 5 pitches/gear to 2.5 inches

From the notch just east of the gendarme, follow the crest of the West Ridge, passing all major obstacles in the form of smaller gendarmes. Climbing up and over the gendarmes greatly increases the difficulty of this climb. The ridge itself becomes narrower and more exposed the higher one climbs. After the first couple of pitches, you will encounter a short, steep, blocky step on the ridge crest (crux). Once past this step, the angle eases and the ridge begins curving toward the blocky summit area. Simul-climbing is an effective method of travel from this point forward or perhaps on the entire route.

Descent: From the summit area, walk south down bear grass slopes and regain the small saddle on the crest just south of the summit. Retrace your steps back along the crest toward Chimney Rock and return the way you came in.

Juli Russell climbs The Fin (5.6) on The High Traverse.

The High Traverse (aka The Beehive Five)

Beehive Dome to Peak 7,171

Number of Routes: One

Grade: IV 5.6

Length: Roughly six miles of mostly 3rd- to 4th-class scrambling plus three pitches of technical climbing

Approach Time: 30 minutes

Climbing Time: 8 to 12 hours

Total Elevation Gain: Over 3,500 feet

Descent Type: Walk-off

Season: Generally June through late September

Maps: USGS The Wigwams (7.5-minute series) or USGS Bonners Ferry (1:100,000-scale metric)

Standing in a picturesque row high on the Selkirk Crest is a string of unnamed peaks – at 7,374 feet, 7,353 feet, 7,167 feet and 7,171 feet – that run due north of Twin Peaks toward Harrison Lake. A truly excellent high route for the savvy mountaineer, a traverse of these peaks is the quintessential Selkirk Crest experience. Distinctly alpine in nature, The High Traverse offers the high-country enthusiast a very long day-trip into the meat of this exceptional mountain range.

The traverse involves many facets of mountain climbing from mild ridge walks to acres of boulder-hopping to a short but very exhilarating and exposed, 5.6 knife-edge ridge climb. All this terminates at the 7,171-foot peak where panoramic views of the region's cardinal points await: British Columbia, Canada, to the north; Washington state to the west; and Montana to the east.

This route requires route-finding skills as well as the ability to scramble unroped across exposed third- and fourth-class terrain in order to complete it in a day. Only fit parties with good mountain sense should attempt to do it in a day. There is no water on the route, except snowmelt in early summer, making the philosophy of "light and fast" very important here. An exit route does exist in the middle of the traverse, making it possible to do the route as a two-part project. Additionally, it is possible to enter the traverse midway simply to do the technical 5.6 knife-edge ridge portion, The Fin. The rock quality on the traverse fluctuates between variable to sound and comes with the usual lather of North Idaho "black lettuce" lichen.

In a mountain range that is not known for its long ridge traverses, this route provides a classic mountaineering adventure in a pristine setting. Look for caribou herds in the basins that flank either side of the traverse. Previous parties have reported sightings of these elusive animals here.

Side Note: The Proposed Selkirk Crest Scenic Trail

Given the truly aesthetic nature of the Selkirk Crest, the author has long dreamed of a well-established – and well-marked – high-country scrambling route that would begin at the Schweitzer Mountain Resort and end just northeast of Red Top Mountain on Smith Creek Road located northwest of Bonners Ferry, Idaho. Such a route would be a multiday affair and would require van or car-shuttling assistance, perhaps a paid service provided by one of the resorts located in Bonners Ferry. The route would begin at Schweitzer Village and climb up to the top of the ski lifts via established trails, then over to Blue Mountain (aka Big Blue).

From here, the proposed Selkirk Crest Scenic Trail would follow the crest in a northerly manner, surmounting Mount Casey, Flat Top, Jeru Peak, Hunt Peak, Gunsight Peak and Mount Roothaan. From the summit of Mount Roothaan, it would drop into the basin on the east side of Chimney Rock and continue along the crest, up and over Silver Dollar Peak, Twin Peaks, the whole length of The High Traverse (as described in this chapter) and then around the north side of the Harrison Lake Cirque. The trail would then traverse the southern flanks of Harrison Peak, wrap around to Myrtle's Turtle, go past Two Mouth Lakes to the cirque just south of Kent Lake, and then cross the ridge crest to Myrtle Peak. From Myrtle Peak the trail would wind along the ridge to the north and then wrap around west to Long Canyon Pass.

From here, a sharp turn south and then west would lead to the Lion's Head Ridge, which would be followed up and over the East Summit of The Lion's Head, followed by a ridge traverse over to Abandoned Mountain, then over to West Fork Mountain, before dropping down into the Caribou Lakes area, past the West Fork cabin, up to Hidden Lake, and finally up and over Red Top and down its northeast ridge to the trailhead on Smith Creek Road. This would be the terminus of the approximately 50-mile trail, which would take most parties four or five days to complete.

How would such a massive trail be built, one might ask? Having worked with various wilderness therapy programs in the area that take youth into the woods for weeks at a time, it seems possible that groups of such students could be employed to work on sections of the trail during the high summer months. Additionally, programs such as Americorps, Outward Bound and other similar programs could assist with the establishment of the trail. All technical portions of the ridge crest (such as the portion described on The High Traverse, page 118) would be skirted so as to create a trail that, while exposed in some areas, would not necessarily require ropes or hardware. Some exposed rock steps

Beehive Dome

HT

might require the placement of hand cables or anchor points for people to lower their backpacks. A 30-foot piece of 1-inch tubular webbing would do the trick here. All in all, this trail would be appropriate for seasoned hikers and scramblers looking to "step up" from such popular trails as the Continental Divide Trail and the Pacific Crest Trail. Permits would be required on the trail and established camping areas would be used. A few bivouacs on rocky perches along the crest would also be possible. Water would need to be collected from small tarns and springs along the way. GPS use would also make sense on a trail of this nature. Emergency bail-out spots would exist along the route, such as around the Chimney Rock, Harrison Lake, Two Mouth Lakes and The Lion's Head areas. If the trail became popular, it could boost summer revenues in both Sandpoint and Bonners Ferry, as well as bring summertime interest to Schweitzer Mountain Resort, which would be the official kickoff point to the trail. Local guiding and outfitting services might also benefit from such a trail.

Getting There (The High Traverse)

Take Highway 95 roughly 13 miles north of Sandpoint, Idaho, and turn left (west) onto the Upper Pack River Road at the gas station. Drive about 20.5 miles (the last 6.5 of which are quite rough)* and park at the Harrison Lake Trail No. 217 trailhead, which is located near the end of the road beside a new vault toilet. This trailhead is also where you will be ending the traverse.

*The Pack River Bridge located 11 miles from the highway washed out in 2006 and will be closed through the 2007 climbing season. Climbers may access the trailhead by any means other than highway vehicles, including mountain bikes or ATVs.

Approach

Begin by walking back down Upper Pack River Road (to the south) for approximately a half mile. The first adventure of the day involves classic North Idaho bushwhacking. Do not let this deter you; it is the only serious bushwhacking of the day. The goal is to locate a spot on the road where the trees thin and you can clearly see a meadow that sits at the base of Beehive Dome – the obvious rock slab situated across the valley to the west. Bushwhack toward the meadow,

Peak 7167'
"The Fin"

To Peak 7171'

THE FIN (5.6), THE HIGH TRAVERSE
HT) The High Traverse (IV 5.6) 3rd and 4th class plus 2 to 3 pitches of 5.6

crossing the Upper Pack River en route. (Note: There is a creek bed that drains off of Beehive Dome in the center of the lower face. This creek bed offers the best approach through the meadow and onto the rock slabs of the dome).

HT) The High Traverse (IV 5.6) Six miles of 3rd- to 4th-class scrambling plus 3 pitches of climbing/small rack with one 3-inch piece

From the base of Beehive Dome, choose a route up the rock slabs that best suits your comfort level. As with most open stretches of slabby rock, it is possible to pick and choose your way upward. Patches of fourth-class can be skirted on the left (south) via easier terrain. Once at the top of Beehive Dome, the terrain levels and turns to bear grass and treed ridges. Hike due west, keeping to the height of land that rises toward the East Ridge of the 7,374-foot peak. Your next goal is to gain the summit of the 7,374-foot peak, which involves a small section of exposed rock directly on the East Ridge.

From the summit of the 7,374-foot peak, look north and familiarize yourself with your horizons (a map is handy here). The ridgeline stretching north is the Selkirk Crest. The high points along this ridge are labeled as Peaks 7,353', 7,167' and 7,171' on the USGS "The Wigwams" map. These are the peaks that you will be traversing.

From the 7,374-foot peak, descend to the northwest via the broken crest and some exposure. From this point on, the name of the game is to stick as close to the ridge crest as possible, choosing the line of least resistance. Once you have gained the 7,353-foot peak, take another moment to review your surroundings. The next major obstacle to the north is the 7,167-foot peak, aka The Fin. This is where the technical climbing portion begins. Near the base of The Fin, you will be confronted by a large gendarme sitting on the ridge crest. Portions of the ridge prior to this gendarme are best passed on the left (west) via third-class ledge systems. The gendarme itself, however, is best passed by locating a sloping ledge system just east of, but below, the top of the gendarme. A small pine tree marks this ledge system. Walk north across the ledge and peer off the gendarme's north side. Careful down-climbing and spotting will bring you through a brief fourth-class step and onto a relatively flat ridge near the base of The Fin. Note: This area marks a potential exit point for parties not interested in continuing up and over The Fin. To exit, down-climb off the east side of the ridge crest and walk overland in a northeasterly manner all the way down to Harrison Lake. Bushwhacking is inevitable. It is also possible to continue along The High Traverse by down-climbing off the ridge crest and regaining The High Traverse just north of The Fin.

If climbing The Fin (highly recommended), continue walking the flat-topped ridge crest just north of the previously mentioned gendarme, using caution on exposed steps in the crest. Most parties will want to rope up at a point where The Fin begins to rise steeply and the ridge thins down to a few feet wide. At the first major step in The Fin, traverse out right (east) for a few feet, step around a blind corner and attack the remainder of the step directly. The remainder of the climb is done on the crest of The Fin with a crux portion involving a wide crack (3 inches) and a very exciting and exposed move up and over it. Belay near the summit.

From the summit of The Fin (7,167 feet), scramble north down slabs and enter boulder fields and trees, which characterize the next portion of the traverse. Pick and choose your way through the boulder fields, heading in the general direction of the 7,171-foot peak. Summit via a scramble up the South Ridge of the 7,171-footer.

Descent: Work down the East Ridge of the 7,171-foot peak via ledge systems. Partway down the ridge, locate a place where it is possible to drop directly north via ledges and enter the basin below. Hike down the basin. (Take care not to trend too far to hiker's right or you will get cliffed out.) Pick your way down to the southwestern shores of Harrison Lake and hike the Harrison Lake trail (found near the outlet stream on the southern edge of the lake) down to your vehicle at the trailhead.

Harrison Peak ___ _ _ _ _ _ _

Harrison Peak (7,292 feet)

Number of Routes: Six known

Grade Range: 5.7 to 5.9

Length Range: 1 to 3 pitches

Approach Time: 2.5 to 3 hours

Climbing Time: 2 to 4 hours

Total Elevation Gain (car to summit): 2,546 feet

Descent Type: Walk-off

Season: Generally June through late September

Maps: USGS The Wigwams (7.5-minute series) or USGS Bonners Ferry (1:100,000-scale metric)

The sight of Harrison Peak hovering above its namesake lake at the headwaters of the Pack River provides one of the loveliest backdrops in all of North Idaho. The Harrison Lake Basin (aka The Harrison Cirque) is a perfect example of the influence glacial ice has on the shape of granite. Thousands of years ago, glaciers ripped through this region, leaving behind the dramatic rock scenery that is seen today.

Access to Harrison Peak is via Upper Pack River Road, a somewhat rough and weather-beaten Forest Service road. At the time of printing, high-clearance vehicles were recommended; however, four-wheel drive was not essential to get to the Harrison Lake trailhead. Despite the road's deteriorating condition, the short 2-mile hike into Harrison Lake is via a well-maintained trail and is one of the most popular hikes into the Selkirk Range. As with all areas covered in this book, human impact at Harrison Lake is becoming an increasingly difficult issue for the Forest Service to manage. It is very important to brush up on Leave No Trace principles provided in this book if planning to visit this area.

Harrison Peak is an aesthetic, granite wedge with a distinct, beak-like summit and a sweeping South Face. The majority of the multipitch, alpine rock-climbing on Harrison Peak is on the South Face, or the Southeast Buttress, both of which are viewed from the approach trail or from high points around Harrison Lake. A handful of one-pitch routes are located on the peak's less visible West Face.

Getting from the lake to the base of Harrison Peak is a stiff, overland mountain ramble. Route-finding skills and good mountain sense are valuable when trying to link the various climber's trails that are picked up near the southeast edge of the lake.

Climbers will find that the rock on Harrison Peak gets progressively better the higher one climbs. The top pitches of both the Standard Route and the Keystone Route provide excellent granite challenges with excellent crack and corner systems. While highly enjoyable, it should be noted that the routes on Harrison Peak are relatively short (three pitches at the most). It is very common to climb several routes in a single, car-to-car day from the trailhead. In fact, a motivated team can sample the entire peak by climbing a route on the South Face, followed by a route on the Southwest Buttress, then rappelling off the summit blocks to tackle the classic Sunset Dihedral (5.9) on the West Face. Other parties, however, may find it a struggle simply to bag the Standard Route and hike back down to the car before dark. If you are planning to climb the peak as a day trip, it is essential that you allow yourself a few extra minutes to hang out at the lake after your climb. A brisk plunge into this spectacular high-country lake is an extraordinary experience that may be the highlight of your trip to North Idaho.

Camping
Car camping at the Harrison Lake trailhead is a very common way to stage day-trip assaults into Harrison Peak. However, backcountry camping at Harrison Lake is an excellent way to fit in numerous routes on the peak over the span of a couple of days. Please note that Harrison Lake is also a possible base camp for climbers trying to climb The Fin (see The High Traverse). A fantastic overnight trip itinerary in the area might include one day spent climbing a few routes on Harrison Peak followed by a second day on The Fin. Add a fly rod into the mix, and you are looking at a fabulous high-country weekend in one of the prettiest parts of the Selkirk Range.

Getting There
Take Highway 95 roughly 13 miles north of Sandpoint, Idaho, and turn left (west) onto Upper Pack River Road at the gas station. Drive about 20.5 miles (the last 6.5 of which are quite rough)* to the Harrison Lake Trail No. 217 trail-head, which is located near the end of the road beside a nice, new vault toilet.

*The Pack River Bridge located 11 miles from the highway washed out in 2006 and will be closed through the 2007 climbing season. Climbers may access the trailhead by any means other than highway vehicles, including mountain bikes or ATVs.

Approach
The trail up to Harrison Lake is about 2.3 miles long and is well-maintained. Once at the lake, hike around to its eastern edge and pick up a climber's trail that rises steeply up the wooded ridge east of the lake. Good views of the South Face of Harrison Peak can be seen once you top out on the ridge. The name of the game here is to continue following the ridge in a northerly direction toward talus fields located on the west side of Harrison Peak. It may seem possible to drop down into the little basin to the east, below the south face, but this is not recommended. Instead, stay as high as possible on the wooded ridge above the lake, enter talus fields just west of the peak and traverse directly east toward the base of the South Face. Some boulder hopping and route finding across slabs and ledges will be encountered along this portion of the approach. Game trails, some flagging tape and a few cairns should be followed if encountered along the way.

Juli Russell on the South Face Left (Standard Route) variation

South Face

All routes are described left to right looking at the face.

MI) Mistaken Identity (5.10+) 2 pitches/gear to 5 inches

The South Face of the peak extends west along a ridge crest with a large blocky gendarme. Mistaken Identity is the obvious wide crack that splits the gendarme.

Pitch 1: Follow cracks and flakes directly below the gendarme. Belay in an alcove just below the wide crack that splits the upper portion of the formation.

Pitch 2: Aid into the overhanging slot (free at 5.10?) and climb it to the top of the ridge.

Descent: Walk the ridge crest to the west until it is possible to circle back down to the South Face.

GE) Gendarme East (5.8) 2 pitches/gear to 3 inches

The right-hand edge of the aforementioned gendarme forms a large dihedral. To the right of this corner is a series of flakes that leads up to the ridge crest.

Pitch 1: Climb up and to the right of the gendarme, then work up slabs to the left toward a notch below the ridge.

Pitch 2: Jam an awkward crack just below the ridge until you gain the ridge crest.

Descent: Down-climb off the north side of the ridge and walk west via ledges until it is possible to pop back up over the ridge and circle back around to the South Face.

SL) South Face Left (Standard Route) (5.7+) 3 pitches/gear to 3 inches

An excellent route, this line climbs up the gut of the south face via nice flake and crack system and joins with the right variation at the crux corner system.

Pitch 1: The middle of the South Face is characterized by black, overlapping waves of granite with a few bushes on them. Just left of these dark overlaps is a series of clean, white slabs with several different cracks and left-facing flake systems. The first pitch begins on an obvious ledge system directly below a thin, white, curving flake. Climb this flake up through a small overlap and into another curving flake section. Continue up discontinuous flakes and cracks to a large, triangular-shaped rock horn, and belay from a small ledge beneath an obvious left-facing corner (clean, white and polished).

Pitch 2: Climb the left-facing corner that ends at some mossy ledges with a few trees. Move up and right at this point, aiming for a gnarly, old, dead tree with seasonal slings wrapped around it.

Pitch 3: This beautiful crux pitch climbs a wide, left-facing corner above the dead tree belay toward an obvious, blocky corner system (crux), which splits the looming headwall above. Power up the crux corner via stellar lieback moves on good granite. After about 20 feet of continuous liebacking, the corner begins trending up and right. Continue up right into a second, shorter corner, which leads to further rightward traversing and eventually ends at the summit ridge just shy of the top. Descend via the gentle east slopes.

SR) South Face Right (Standard Route) (5.7+) 3 pitches/gear to 3 inches

This variation climbs to the right of the previously mentioned route; its lower pitches are easier, a bit dirtier, but still offer several challenging and fun climbing situations.

Pitch 1: Just right of the clean, white slabs and flakes on the first pitch of the left variation, locate a series of corners (darker and a bit dirtier) that lead up and right. Climb any one of a series of these corners to a ledge system out right with a dead tree on it.

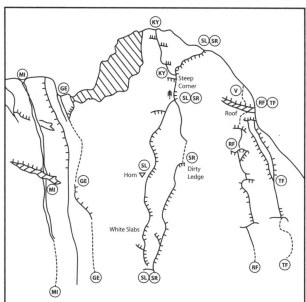

HARRISON PEAK

MI) Mistaken Identity (5.10+)
GE) Gendarme East (5.8)
SL) South Face Left (Standard Route) (II 5.7+)
SR) South Face Right (Standard Route) (II 5.7+)
KY) Keystone Route (5.9)
RF) Running Flakes (II 5.8)
V) Direct Finish Variation (5.9)
TF) Twin Flakes (II 5.8)
WF) West Face Flake (5.7+)
SD) Sunset Dihedral (5.9)
D) Descent (Walk Off)

Pitch 2: Continue above via a ridge-like formation just right of center on the face that leads to a gnarly, old, dead tree with seasonal slings wrapped around it.

Pitch 3: This beautiful crux pitch climbs a wide, left-facing corner above the dead tree belay toward an obvious, blocky corner system (crux), which splits the looming headwall above. Power up the crux corner via stellar lieback moves on good granite. After about 20 feet of continuous liebacking, the corner begins trending up and right. Continue up right into a second, shorter corner that leads to further rightward traversing and eventually ends at the summit ridge just shy of the top. Descend via the gentle east slopes.

KY) Keystone Route (5.9) 1 pitch/Fixed pitons plus gear to 2 inches

This excellent direct finish to the South Face Standard Routes is highly recommended for those confident at the grade. Steep blocks and fun, exposed moves charge up through the daunting headwall that caps the upper South Face.

To access this pitch, climb the initial corner systems on the third pitch of the Standard Route. However, instead of traversing out right after the first 20 feet of strenuous liebacking, move up and left via face climbing and mantle onto a ledge directly below the summit area. A few tricky moves past a piton leads into steep blocks that are climbed directly to the top.

Southeast Buttress

Roughly 150 yards to the right (east) of the South Face is a protruding buttress characterized by many overlapping flakes and some lichen-covered rock. This is known collectively as the Southeast Buttress.

RF) Running Flakes (5.8) 3 pitches/gear to 3 inches

This route begins on a patch of white and gray rock just left of center on the main portion of the buttress.

Pitch 1: Climb slabs and discontinuous cracks up to a right-facing flake system. Continue up the flake to a small belay platform.

Pitch 2: Climb up and slightly left through a small system of dihedrals. Halfway up the pitch, climb through a small roof to the rock cornice that makes up Harrison Peak's southeastern skyline. Belay from a stance directly under the far right edge of the rock cornice.

Pitch 3: Reach blindly up and around the far right side of the rock cornice. A secret jug leads to easy mantles and, eventually, the summit ridge.

V) Direct Finish Variation (5.9) 1 pitch/gear to 2 inches

From the top of the second pitch on Running Flakes, climb a shallow, curving crack directly above the second-pitch belay ledge toward a short, steep wall in the middle of the massive roof above. Place a small TCU at the base of the wall and reach high above, over the top of the wall and locate a tiny in-cut micro pocket. Yank on this to surmount the wall, mantle onto the ledge and then scramble to the top.

Descent: As for the South Face Standard Route.

TF) Twin Flakes (5.8) 3 pitches/gear to 3 inches

Fifty feet right of Running Flakes, locate a pair of flakes that face each other high on the wall. These double flakes are encountered on the second pitch of the route.

Pitch 1: Climb directly up a left-facing flake and then stem out right into a right-facing flake. Near the top of the flake, climb out left to a belay stance below the obvious double flakes.

Pitch 2: Climb the double flakes directly up to the rock cornice and belay on its far right side.

Pitch 3: Reach blindly up and around the far right side of the rock cornice. A secret jug leads to easy mantles and, eventually, the summit ridge.

Descent: As for the South Face Standard Route.

Thad Laird on the crux corner pitch of the South Face Standard Route on Harrison Peak

West Face

Gaining the West Face is best done by climbing one of the routes on the South Face or Southeast Buttress. From the summit of Harrison Peak, walk 15 feet north and drop down to a small, white, gravelly ledge. Look down the West Face and notice an obvious, right-facing corner system directly below. This is the Sunset Dihedral. Build an anchor here and perform a double-rope rappel down to the base of the route. From this point, you can access the other routes on the West Face. Once back on the summit, clean the rappel anchor you made and descend as for the South Face Standard Route.

WF) West Face Flake (5.7+) 1 pitch/gear to 3 inches

This route climbs a series of cracks, flakes and blocks on the far left side of the West Face. Aim just left of a prominent notch near the summit area. Climb a small dihedral that leads to a mantle move and larger flakes. Climb up behind a large flake and blocks with a cave. Go left behind the block or face climb up and right to the summit.

SD) Sunset Dihedral (5.9) 1 pitch/gear to 3 inches

This clean open book is located directly below the summit area. Begin by chimneying up through a slot to gain access to the stellar dihedral. Stem up the corner via finger cracks and some strenuous lieback moves to the top.

Myrtle's Turtle

Myrtle's Turtle (Peak 6,482 feet)

Number of Routes: Unknown

Grade: II+ 5.5

Length: 6 to 7 pitches

Approach Time: 2 hours

Climbing Time: 3 to 4 hours

Total Elevation Gain (car to summit): 1,682 feet

Descent Type: Walk-off

Season: Generally June through late September

Maps: USGS The Wigwams (7.5-minute series) or USGS Bonners Ferry (1:100,000-scale metric)

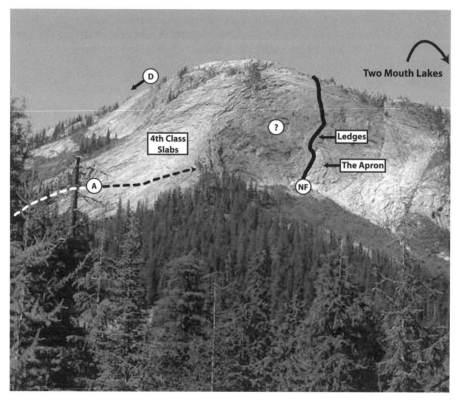

MYRTLE'S TURTLE
A) Approach via Upper Myrtle Creek
NF) North Face Standard Route (II+ 5.5) 6-7 pitches
?) Unknown routes may exist
D) Descent (Walk Off)

Myrtle's Turtle has been a landmark destination for hikers, rock scramblers and backcountry skiers for years. Sitting on a high perch overlooking the Upper Myrtle Creek drainage just east of Two Mouth Lakes, Myrtle's Turtle (aka Peak 6,482 feet) is distinctly granite in color and shape: a massive blob of white rock born from the Kaniksu Batholith. While a majority of Myrtle's Turtle is gentle and rounded (and thus of interest to area hikers and skiers), the looming north face holds excellent climbing possibilities.

As with many North Idaho climbing objectives, getting to the base of the Turtle is not an easy endeavor. Bushwhacking and route-finding are necessary skills to employ. But if you are thinking of foregoing a trip to this formation due to this fact, please rethink. The approach is steep and brushy but is not excessively long and leads to some of the most fun slab climbing in the area.

The history of rock climbing on Myrtle's Turtle is a tough thing to gauge. As is the standard while researching guidebooks, unreturned phone calls and several dead ends posed difficult obstacles while trying to garner information about climbs on this peak. With spotty beta scribbled into a notebook and a keen desire to reach the clean, upper-slab pitches rumored to be on the North Face, the author groveled into the Turtle, chose what appeared to be the most obvious weakness up the North Face and strung together a series of cracks, ledges and yes, very clean, white slabs, to the top. From this ascent, as well as from beta offered by friends who have been hiking and skiing in the area for years, the author has labeled the ascent the North Face Standard Route. Needless to say, there are undoubtedly numerous other routes that have been climbed over the years. It was not the author's intent to simply overlook or avoid documenting these climbs; this information was simply not found.

The route described here is fun and moderate and, as you will find, terminates in tremendous views of some of the loveliest high country in the entire Gem State.

Getting There

In Bonners Ferry, Idaho (roughly 31 miles north of Sandpoint), turn west off Highway 95 next to the Kootenai River bridge onto Riverside Street and head toward the Kootenai National Wildlife Refuge. After about 5.4 miles, turn right on Westside Road past the wildlife refuge headquarters. Go about 1.3 miles to Myrtle Creek Road No. 633. Turn left and drive just over 12 miles to where Road No. 633 becomes Road No. 661 at the Two Mouth Lakes trailhead. At this point, the North Face of Myrtle's Turtle is clearly visible on the ridge in front of you. Continue along Road 661 for about 1.5 miles to the junction with Road No. 2409. Turn right and follow Road No. 2409 (toward the Upper Myrtle Creek Trail No. 6 trailhead) for roughly one mile, until you notice an opening in the trees to the west that allows one to see the East Face of the Turtle high above. The goal is to locate an avalanche gully, which looks like a ski run in the summertime, that leads up to the base of some gray slabs high on the ridge. Park on the side of the road where it is most convenient. (Note: If you continue along this road it eventually dead-ends at the trailhead for Upper Myrtle Creek).

Approach

While relatively short in terms of overall distance, the approach to the North Face of Myrtle's Turtle is not easy. It involves classic North Idaho off-trail hiking

East Face

MYRTLE'S TURTLE A) Approach to North Face via Upper Myrtle Creek

(Read: bushwhacking) as well as route-finding skills. The time-honored tradition of pack-stashing partway up the approach is highly recommended. This is due to the fact that the descent route (via the East Face) crosses paths with the approach route. If you are not inclined to perform a pack-stash, it is advised to do a carry-over on the climbing route so that you don't have to go all the way back around to the North Face to fetch your caboodle after the climb.

From the car, hike west (downhill at first) through the bush toward the Upper Myrtle Creek drainage, which is crossed via wading or careful rock hopping. Proceed through open grass toward the obvious avalanche gully that tumbles down from the East Face of Myrtle's Turtle. It is generally best to follow the right-hand (north) edge of the avalanche gully, which has a small stream snaking down it. The terrain is steep on this right-hand bank but relatively bush-free. A third of the way up, however, the alder begins to set in. It may be best to work into the stream bottom itself so as to avoid the heavier brush, but a direct shot through the alders is possible. The upper slopes of the gully are quite steep, but the brush thins down into a potpourri of bramble, huckleberry

MYRTLE'S TURTLE NF) North Face Standard Route (II+ 5.5) 6 to 7 pitches. This image shows the first pitch of the route.

and bear grass. Once you are within a few hundred yards of the slabby, gray cliffs of the East Face, begin traversing to the right (north), crossing brush slopes and exposed rock until you come to the toe of the northeast slabs: a very obvious series of open, smooth, white slabs. Cross these slabs low and descend to the north via gully systems, curving around to the North Face. In the center of the lower North Face, notice a bulging slab formation the shape of a rock "apron." This apron is easily visible as you walk toward it along the base of the face (refer to the photo above).

NF) North Face Standard Route (5.5) 6 to 7 pitches/gear to 3 inches

Once you have located The Apron, notice that the left side of it is characterized by an obvious, wide crack/corner system. Just right of this corner system, on the apron itself, is a series of low-angle, polished slabs. The route begins by scampering up these slabs.

Pitch 1: Motor up low-angle slabs (5.2 at the most) on the far left side of The Apron, passing through small, granite overlaps with bits of pro here and there. Climb a full 200-foot (60-meter) pitch to a series of small, slanting ledges partway up The Apron. Engineer an anchor among the blank granite slabs, and belay.

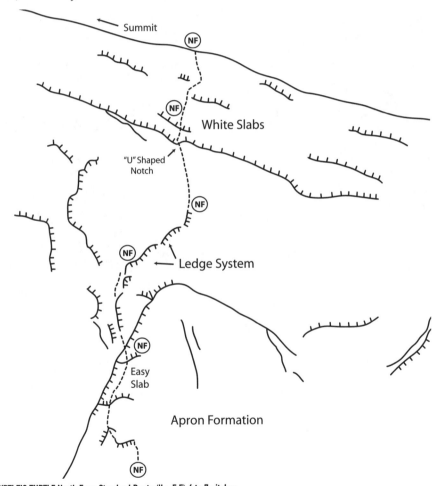

MYRTLE'S TURTLE North Face Standard Route (II+ 5.5) 6 to 7 pitches

Pitch 2: This crux pitch requires exiting The Apron via a leftward traverse, crossing over the wide crack/corner system that makes up The Apron's left side and climbing a series of left-facing corners to a broad ledge that slashes across the face. The corners involve pleasant liebacking up to a small roof, which is passed on the right. Continue up to the major, right-trending ledge system. Belay from a small stance on the left edge of the ledge system. (Note: From this belay, it should be obvious that the terrain directly above you is harder than 5.5 and that the ledge system running out to climber's right is, by far, the path of least resistance).

Pitches 3 and 4: Climb the ledge system out right, traversing past flakes and overlaps. The ledge is generally easy except for a few protruding sections, which are passed via ledges below them or by stemming up and over them. After roughly a pitch and a half, the entire layout of the North Face comes into view and you realize that you are now smack in the center of the face. At this point, look up and review the upper skyline. It is important to locate a unique U-shaped notch in the horizon. Move up toward this notch via a clean swath of granite that splits a bushy section. Belay on the slabs directly below the notch. These pitches are the least interesting or aesthetic but set you up for the money pitches above.

Juli Russell on the amazing upper slab pitches, North Face Standard Route

Pitch 5: Tiptoe up the slabs toward the unique U-shaped notch in the horizon. Punch up through the notch via a fun mantle (good pro on the lip of the notch) and continue another 30 feet or so to an obvious, horizontal crack running across the face. Use the crack for a belay anchor. From here on, the climbing goes from neat to spectacular as you continue up beautiful sheets of blank granite, searching (mostly in vain) for protection. But not to worry, difficulties rarely exceed low fifth-class on these upper slabs.

Pitch 6: Dance up the clean, white slabs, aiming for any obvious weaknesses and engineering pro when you can. A variety of exit strategies exist, but it may be best to trend up and left near the top, aiming for a large corner system near some massive pine trees on the upper skyline. Belay just below the summit plateau area, which is a soccer field-sized portion of granite with stunning views of the Selkirk Crest and Two Mouth Lakes below.

Descent: Hike up and over the bulging summit area. If you stashed your pack at the base of the East Face, or are performing a carry-over (highly recommended), your next adventure is to continue hiking in an easterly manner, trending south when the terrain gets too steep. The name of the game is to curl around beneath the East Face. Some rope work or careful spotting may be required for less-confident parties. Once you reach the bottom of the East Face, retrace your footsteps down through the approach gully to the car. If you still have gear to retrieve at the base of the North Face, it is possible to scamper down the northeast slabs directly off the summit area and then curl back around to the base of the North Face. (Note: Do not attempt to descend the massive avalanche gully located directly north of the peak. The author made this mistake and spent three hours bushwhacking through horrendous alder and fending off mosquitoes the size of small birds).

The Lion's Head (West Peak)

The Lion's Head (West Peak 7,226 feet)

Number of Routes: Unknown

Grade Range: 5.4 to 5.10 A3

Length Range: 3 to 5 pitches (south and east aspects) or 6 to 8 pitches (north aspects)

Approach Time: 2 to 3 hours

Climbing Time: 1 to 4 hours (south aspects) or 4 to 10+ hours (north aspects)

Total Elevation Gain (car to summit): 2,626 feet

Descent Type: 2 to 3 single-rope (60-meter) rappels

Season: Generally June through late September

Maps: USGS Smith Peak (7.5-minute series) or USGS Bonners Ferry (1:100,000-scale metric)

In the second chapter of John Roskelley's reflective essay on mountaineering called "Stories Off the Wall," he describes his early years of climbing in North Idaho with his inseparable climbing buddy Bob Christianson. Among the duo's notable accomplishments was the first ascent of the North Face of The Lion's Head. In his book, Roskelley mentions the climb only briefly, explaining that the team attempted it in 1969 after a horrendous approach and a forced bivouac partway up the 800-foot face.

For decades, this brief mention of climbing routes on the twin summits of The Lion's Head were shrouded in mystery and legend. Rumors of untapped route potential and big, scary free climbs were exchanged from bar stools at Eichardt's Pub and Grill in Sandpoint. Only a handful of people actually knew a handful of people who had once visited the peak. A confirmed story of someone actually scaling the thing was as elusive as the mountain itself.

In the summer of 2002, however, everything changed. While enjoying a conversation with a group of Spokane climbers at the Mount Roothaan trailhead, a different type of story regarding The Lion's Head surfaced. These climbers claimed to have actually set foot on the mountain itself on several occasions over the past few years. Comments such as "an easy approach" and "We did it as a day trip from Spokane" began dropping from their mouths. As I sat there listening – wide-eyed and entertained by the fury of hand gestures taking to the air, I began to realize that, like most things in life, The Lion's Head was probably not nearly as daunting as the legends had made it out to be.

Two weeks later, I was standing chest-deep in devil's club (a thorny, ferocious willywhack for those who have yet to make its acquaintance) wishing I had taken better notes on the "easy approach" they had mentioned. During the drive in, my climbing partner and I had caught site of the impressive North Face of the West Peak of The Lion's Head. Neither of us had seen anything of its kind in the North Idaho Selkirks before. It reminded us of walls we had climbed over in the North Cascades of Washington state. Once we found the proper climber's trail, which leads up from Abandoned Creek into the broad basin beneath the mountain's sheer North Face, it was obvious that we had found something unique.

Later that afternoon, having established camp on the west side of the West Peak, I took off on a solo stroll to scout the Southern Slabs route, which were reported by the Spokane climbers as being the quickest, easiest way to the top. Once at the base of the slabs, I suddenly had one of those notions that "just scrambling up a few feet" of the route would be a good idea. I tossed on my climbing shoes, tied my rope to my back and began edging up the unknown slabs. The higher I climbed, the more I was drawn into the mountain. An hour later I was standing on the summit.

As the sun steadily dipped below the western horizon, I recalled something the Spokane climbers had mentioned. They had said that the summit register located in the massive summit cairn held the Holy Grail of climbing information regarding The Lion's Head. So I extracted this historical relic gingerly, as if performing an archeological dig. Inside the box were several slips of old paper, a tiny notebook, a small cylindrical metal tube, and a couple old pencils. Inside the metal tube was a faded piece of paper. Scribbled on it was a barely visible date: 1938. It was the first recorded ascent of the peak made by a man from Bonners Ferry, Idaho, during a time when my grandfather was just a boy. Large gaps of time separated all subsequent climbs of the peak. There were a few scribbles from the 1970s, then a big gap until the '80s and then a larger concentration of notes starting around the turn of the millennium by the Spokane climbers I had met at the Mount Roothaan trailhead. This was the missing link to the legend. I scribbled a few route notes onto a slip of paper, tucked it into my pocket, rappelled the slabs and was back at camp a minute shy of darkness. And needless to say, this was not to be my last encounter with the sentinel block of rock known as The Lion's Head.

History

Most of the routes described here are the old classics of the peak – climbs that have seen numerous repeats and grade agreements. However, as you will notice, some of the faces included here are simply marked with question marks. This is due to the fact that no specific information beyond basic grades and locations have been confirmed. The main thing climbers need to know about climbing on The Lion's Head is that all known climbs of the mountain have been recorded in the summit register located in a small gray metal box stuffed inside the massive summit cairn.

New route information has been steadily added in the 2000s by a handful of local climbers, namely Dan Swanson and his pal Wayne (last name unknown). However, these routes have not been confirmed by third parties, and therefore many of them have not been included in this book. It is hoped that concrete information on new route activity can be relayed in further editions of this book. Please respect the information in the summit register as a gift. Do not remove any of the information or objects from the register. This is a tangible piece of North Idaho's rock climbing history.

Camping

For single-day assaults on The Lion's Head, car camping at the hairpin turn (see the "Getting There" section) or camping at an established campground on the east side of Priest Lake, are the best options. However, for those in the mood, backcountry camping can be done on large (house-sized) boulders beneath the West Peak's West Face, or at a point where the initial approach trail meets the large boulder field beneath the North Face. Be prepared for very primitive conditions here. Water may be an issue under the West Face in late summer.

Amenities

There is a café/store in the township of Coolin that offers excellent shakes, burgers, a small assortment of groceries and canned goods, pop and other beverages. Beer can be purchased for take-away at the neighboring bar. For those with extra time and a need for a real meal, drive around to the west side of Priest Lake and follow Highway 57 north to the town of Nordman.

Emergency Facilities

The closest pay phone is located in the township of Coolin. However, Newport, Washington, roughly 36 miles southwest of Coolin on Highway 2, offers the closest emergency facilities.

Getting There

From the town of Priest River, Idaho, drive north on Highway 57 for approximately 23 miles and turn right (east) toward the township of Coolin. Go about 5.25 miles to Coolin and turn right (east) onto Cavanaugh Bay Road. Travel another three miles or so and veer right onto East Shore Road. Drive for roughly 23.5 miles along the east shore of Priest Lake and turn right (east) onto Forest Service Road No. 44. After a few miles, Road No. 44 begins switchbacking, steeply at times, and eventually gains a small valley where the road levels off and straightens out. Along this stretch of road, you will see the North Face of the West Peak of The Lion's Head rising above the treetops. Shortly thereafter, Road No. 44 curves to the left and crosses a small creek (Abandoned Creek). Immediately after crossing this creek, a side road veers off right. Take this road and proceed for several hundred yards until you come to a hairpin turn. Park at this hairpin. (Note: Continuing around the hairpin should bring you to a locked gate anyhow.)

Approach

From the hairpin turn, hike due south along an old roadbed located above Abandoned Creek. After about a half mile, notice a side trail (well flagged) leading off to the left (east). This is the main climber's trail that has gone from horrible to manageable over the past few years as the peak becomes more popular with hikers and the occasional rock climber. Be on the lookout for patches of devil's club along this steep climber's trail, and, as always, make plenty of noise so as to avoid a sudden encounter with an unsuspecting bear.

Follow the climber's trail up through the bush for about an hour until the North Face of the West Peak comes clearly into view above you. At this point, you enter a large boulder field that sits at the base of the North Face. If you are planning to climb the Lion Tamer (III 5.10), or any other routes on the northern aspects of the West Peak, this is a great place to stop and plot your heroic siege upon its ominous flanks. Dogs, extra water bottles and extra clothing or gear can be stashed here.

If you are heading to the west, south or east aspects of the peak, look to the right (west) of the North Face and notice a broad, timbered shoulder leading off to the west. Your next challenge involves crossing the basin via boulder hopping and aiming for this shoulder with grand hopes that you will be able to sprint directly up it and deposit yourself under the mountain's West Face with little struggling. In reality, this feat is fairly difficult. The author can testify to several occasions where he found himself attacking this "tiny, insignificant little shoulder" directly, only to find himself pasted to steep, wet, fifth-class terrain and clawing at clumps of moss as he slowly slipped from the cliff side. Needless to say, it is highly recommended that you add 15 minutes to your approach by skirting farther right (west) beneath the steep shoulder, and locating a series of ledges and gully systems that bring you to the top of the shoulder with much less consequence. Once you have gained the shoulder, continue circumnavigating the peak (now beneath its West Face) via a bit of bushwhacking and more boulder hopping. Your next destination is a spur ridge that runs in a southwesterly direction off the southern edge of the peak. On this ridge is a large (garage-sized) gendarme that becomes clearly visible as you approach the ridge. Gain the ridge near the gendarme. The Southern Slabs (II 5.4 R) are the series of down-sloping slabs rising above the ridge. If approaching The Southeast Faces or The East Buttress, proceed on game trails below the South Face to your intended route. These trails eventually lead to the saddle between the West and East Peaks.

Jason Munzke on the East Buttress

East vs. West Peaks

It is important to note that The Lion's Head has two distinct summits, thus giving it the appearance of a crouching lion. The West Peak is where all the real climbing routes are located and is home to the ominous, 800-foot North Face. The higher East Peak has a fun scramble route up its West Ridge, as well as steep east and south aspects that may hold new climbing route potential.

West Peak

EB) East Buttress (5.7) 3 pitches/gear to 2 inches

Gain the exceptional East Buttress by hiking around to the saddle between the West and East Peaks of The Lion's Head (see details on how to reach the saddle in Approach section). Scramble third-class terrain to the base of the buttress proper and belay near a large, dead tree. From this point, locate a large, white corner roughly two-thirds of the way up the buttress. This is The Great White Corner Variation (5.9). The East Buttress follows the buttress crest itself (which looks awfully harder than 5.7 from below).

Pitch 1: Begin in a shallow corner at the base of the buttress that leads up a few feet to a steep wall. Bear right at the wall and curve around into a hand crack just right of the crest. Climb this crack for about 30 feet, until you can swing back left onto the buttress crest beneath a steep bulge. Climb the bulge directly, which is located on the very crest of the buttress. A piton protects a funky move up and over the top of the bulge to a ledge with a large block. Belay here.

Pitch 2: Continue directly up the crest through an unlikely looking bulge with good holds (5.7 at the most). Exit up and left onto a thin section of ridge and belay in a small notch near the summit.

Pitch 3: From the notch, exit up and left via a belly flop move and saunter to the summit.

Descent: Rappel down the Southern Slabs with one 60-meter rope.

GW) The Great White Corner (5.9) 1 pitch/gear to 3 inches

Follow the first pitch of the East Buttress. Instead of veering out left onto the buttress crest partway up the pitch, move up and right into the obvious, white corner. Climb this up and right, curving into the belay notch at the top of the second pitch of the East Buttress. Finish as for that route.

THE LION'S HEAD (WEST PEAK) EAST BUTTRESS
LU) Southeast Face/East Buttress Linkup (III 5.8) 6 pitches
EB) East Buttress (II+ 5.7) 3 pitches
GW) The Great White Corner (5.9)

North Face

NE) Northeast Face (5.7 A2) Pitches Unknown

No further information is available on this route.

LT) The Lion Tamer (5.10) 6 to 7 pitches/gear to 4 inches

Probably the site of the original aid route up the North Face done by John Roskelley and Bob Christianson in 1969, this is a stunning assault up the central weakness of the North Face. The Lion Tamer requires a full range of mountain skills and, as always, an adventurous spirit. This impressive climb requires a strong party and a true love for overcoming difficulties via good mountain sense and perseverance. The rock is quite dirty and loose in spots, but further ascents and perhaps a bit of old-fashioned "elbow grease" will dictate its future quality.

THE LION'S HEAD NORTH FACE
EB) East Buttress (II+ 5.7) 3 pitches
GW) The Great White Corner (5.9)
NE) Northeast Face (III 5.7 A2)
LT) Lion Tamer (III 5.10) 6 to 7 pitches

WF) West Face (Unknown)
CC) Catacombs (II 5.7) 3 pitches
SS) Southern Slabs (II 5.4 R) 3 pitches
SF) South Face (Unknown)
LU) Southeast Face/East Buttress Linkup (III 5.8) 6 pitches

Pitch 1: Locate a loose, left-facing dihedral in the center of the North Face. Delicately climb this wide chimney to a small ledge with a two-piton belay station.

Pitch 2: Choose your own adventure by following easy flakes and crack systems, aiming for a small, bushy ledge above.

Pitch 3: Continue up the obvious crack system, jamming and stemming through a roof into a 5.10 layback crack, which eventually deposits you at a large, treed ledge in the center of the North Face.

Pitch 4: Climb the wide, arching crack to a mantle move that leads to easy face climbing. Position your belay behind a large flake.

Pitch 5: Traverse up and right on thin fingers and hands toward the "Great White Dike." Easy ramp climbing above leads to a large ledge.

Pitch 6: Carefully traverse the ledge out right and up to the summit via easy climbing. An alternate variation is to climb the 5.10 crack directly above.

Descent: Rappel the Southern Slabs with one 60-meter rope.

West Face

WF) West Face (Unknown)

No further information is available about this route. Please refer to the notes located in the summit cairn.

CC) Catacombs (5.7) 3 pitches/gear to 4 inches

An interesting chimney system that sits on the West Face but faces due south. The route is tucked back into a corner at a spot where the West Face bulges out. No further information is available about this route. It looks rather dirty and may stay wet through late summer.

Jason Munzke on the summit of The Lion's Head, West Peak

Southern Aspects

Approach as for the West Face but continue hiking around to the backside (south side) of the peak. Routes described left to right.

SS) Southern Slabs (5.4 R) 3 pitches/gear to 2.5 inches

Directly above the ridge that stretches south and away from The Lion's Head (West Peak), there are a series of blank, gray slabs that offer a quick, fun romp to the summit. Most climbers will opt to scramble up these slabs in order to reach the summit cairn, which holds all route information on the peak. The slabs are climbed from a low point where the southern tip of the slabs drops down toward bear grass slopes at the base of the route.

Pitch 1: A blank, slabby crux move right off the ground leads over a bulge and onto the slabs. From here, climb directly up to a large tree with rappel slings on it.

Pitches 2 and 3: Several options exist. It is possible to climb through the belay tree for a few feet and move out left (west) around the tree and onto a slabby ridge which is climbed to the top. Alternatively, move around to the right (east) of the belay tree and friction up a series of slabs that deposits you at a second tree with slings. (This is the rappel point for descents off the peak).

Descent: Rappel the route with one 60-meter rope.

SF) South Face (Unknown)

No further information is available about this route. Please refer to the notes located in the summit cairn.

LU) Southeast Face/East Buttress Linkup (5.8) 6 pitches/gear to 3 inches

On the far right (east) side of the South Face, notice an obvious slab at the base of the rock covered in lime-green lichen. The right side of this slab is dominated by a large, protruding buttress (the Southeast Buttress). Directly above the green-lichen slab, locate a double-crack system. This is the money pitch on the Southeast Face.

Pitch 1: Motor up the slab covered in pretty, green lichen. Pro is sparse, but the climbing is easy. Continue up into a left-trending ramp/corner system that ends at a steep corner below the obvious double cracks. Climb up into the double cracks, jamming and stemming and loving life. A slab above leads up and left to the base of an obvious dihedral. Belay here.

Pitch 2: Climb the obvious dihedral (thin pro) which is clean and classic. Once the dihedral ends, exit up and right via a steep face with good holds. The name of the game is to traverse directly up and right and gain a notch in the right skyline. Continuing up left gets you into unsavory terrain with down-sloping rock and teetering boulders. It should be obvious that one must avoid these mountain features by traversing directly out right to the aforementioned notch in the skyline. An exposed move across a slab leads to the notch. Belay here.

Pitch 3: Move the belay directly right until you gain the bottom of the East Buttress.

Pitches 4 to 6: Continue up the East Buttress route to the summit.

THE LION'S HEAD (WEST PEAK), SOUTHERN ASPECTS
LU) Southeast Face/East Buttress Linkup (III 5.8) 6 pitches

THE LION'S HEAD (East Peak) WS) West Slabs (4th Class)

East Peak

West Slabs (4th Class)

The west-facing slabs on the East Peak of The Lion's Head offer a fun mountain scramble climbed from the saddle between the West Peak and East Peak. From the saddle, scramble up smooth, down-sloping slabs. Angle left near the top to gain brushy slopes just below the summit. A large summit cairn and a summit register are located at the top. Great views looking back at the monstrous West Peak makes this scramble well worth the effort. Down-climb the route back to the saddle between the East Peak and West Peak.

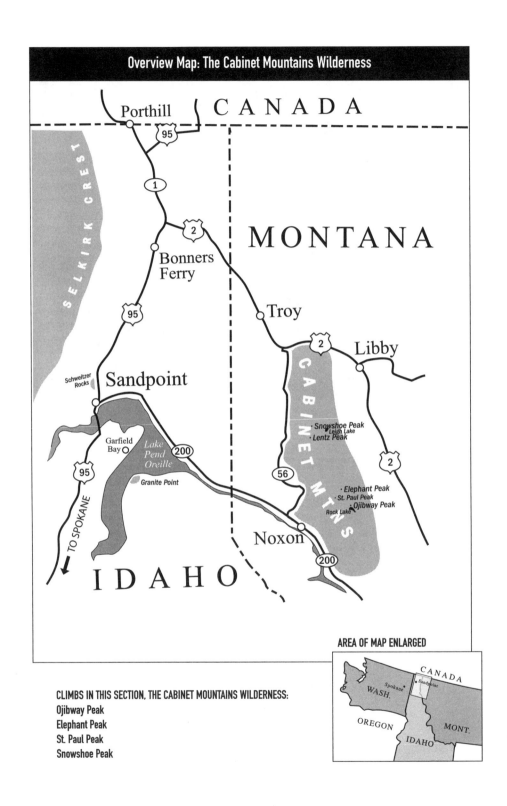

Overview Map: The Cabinet Mountains Wilderness

CANADA

Porthill

MONTANA

Bonners Ferry

Troy

Libby

SELKIRK CREST

Schweitzer Rocks

Sandpoint

CABINET MTNS

Snowshoe Peak
Leigh Lake
Lentz Peak

Garfield Bay

Lake Pend Oreille

Granite Point

Elephant Peak
St. Paul Peak
Ojibway Peak
Rock Lake

TO SPOKANE

Noxon

IDAHO

CLIMBS IN THIS SECTION, THE CABINET MOUNTAINS WILDERNESS:
Ojibway Peak
Elephant Peak
St. Paul Peak
Snowshoe Peak

AREA OF MAP ENLARGED

CANADA
WASH.
Spokane
Sandpoint
OREGON
IDAHO
MONT.

Section III:

The Cabinet Mountains Wilderness

The first thing climbers need to know about climbing in the Cabinet Mountains Wilderness is that these mountains are not the Sierra Nevadas nor the North Cascades. The Cabinets are wild and of distinguishable flavor. These are some of the last great tracts of mountain wilderness left in the Lower 48. This is a place where black bears outnumber tourists; where solitude is a reality, not a fringe benefit; where cell phones are useless; and locals usually carry rifles instead of decorative walking sticks. This is the essence of Montana – a state known for some of the most rugged wilderness left in North America.

The 94,360-acre Cabinet Mountains Wilderness Area is a long, narrow corridor of stunning high country that stretches south from Highway 2 just west of Libby, Montana, to Highway 200 near Noxon, Montana. This Wilderness Area was first preserved as a Primitive Area in 1935 but was upgraded to full Wilderness Area status with the passing of the 1964 Wilderness Act. In fact, the Cabinet Mountains Wilderness was one of 10 areas first designated as Wilderness Areas in this country.

Climbing in the Cabinet Wilderness is what climbing was probably like in the Colorado Rockies 40 years ago. Locals will look at you strangely when they see ropes and helmets and ice axes dangling from your backpack. During early spring assaults, people will inquire about the skis on your feet. During solo treks into this wilderness, it is not uncommon to be the only mammal species capable of speaking. The others must rely on grunting or screeching or the great pounding of hooves as means of communication. Learn to embrace and respect this reality, and you will find some of the greatest mountain challenges of your career.

Additionally, it is strongly recommended to purchase the USGS Elephant Peak, Howard Lake and Snowshoe Peak maps prior to exploring this range. Visiting climbers need to have a strong knowledge of map and compass, route finding, bushwhacking and how to endure long approaches. Those used to obvious trails, bolted anchors and casual descents need to realize that the Cabinets may be a challenging place to climb. However, once you get up on the peaks themselves, you will instantly see why some people choose to hike, climb, ski and enjoy the splendor of this range.

Climbing History

The history of climbing in the Cabinet Range is as elusive as the giant grizzly bears that roam throughout it. Extensive research into first-ascent information, new-route activity and unclimbed faces has resulted in unreturned phone calls, spotty e-mail replies and a general feeling that those who live and climb in this area are perfectly happy not to share it with anyone else.

Let it be stated here that this decision is highly respected by the author. All the pioneers before us have earned the right to keep their routes to themselves.

As a result of this, today's Cabinet Mountains Wilderness climbers are faced with two differing ethics. One ethic is the "Go find it yourself" approach to climbing in the area. The other ethic is the "Let's compile the information together and share it with the rest of the climbing community" approach. While there will never be agreement regarding which ethic is better, members from each school of thought have politely agreed to disagree.

During the summer of 2002, a small group of climbers from the Sandpoint area made it their goal to seek out new or seldom-climbed routes in this range to establish a handful of classics that the rest of us could enjoy. Almost every route described in this section is the result of this effort. These climbers ventured into the Cabinet Wilderness armed with little or no information, because none was available. The goal was to climb several of the obvious mountain features seen during backcountry ski trips or fly-fishing expeditions into the area. Various ridges, arêtes and steep faces were all climbed in the traditional ground-up method, always looking for evidence of climbers past and never truly knowing if the routes below us were first ascents or not. They most likely were not.

This said, please note that the route information compiled in this section is entirely one-sided and does not take into account any other previous ascents because that information was not made available for this book. The one main exception to this has been information provided by Himalayan veteran John Roskelley who provided as much information as he could remember about his early days exploring this region. Indeed, one simply needs to refer to Roskelley's triumphant book "Stories Off the Wall" and flip through the color photos provided to see a young, fit Roskelley framed against the dramatic backdrop of Ojibway Peak in the Cabinet Mountains Wilderness.

No matter what ethic you adhere to, please remember that a strict, no-bolting rule applies to all climbing in the Cabinet Mountains Wilderness. This is not an ethic: This a rule set forth by the region's governing agencies. Pitons have been found on some of the more obvious lines and were left undisturbed as historical evidence of previous ascents. If planning to overnight in the range, always come equipped with a working knowledge of the Leave No Trace philosophy. This range is one of the last pristine ranges in North America. Do whatever it takes to ensure this does not change.

Ojibway Peak

Ojibway Peak (7,303 feet)

Number of Routes: Four known

Grade Range: 5.7 to 5.9

Length Range: 5 to 6 pitches

Approach Time: 3 hours

Climbing Time: 3 to 6 hours

Total Elevation Gain (car to summit): 4,099 feet

Descent Type: Walk-off (some minor down-climbing)

Season: Generally June through late September

Maps: USGS Elephant Peak and Howard Lake (7.5-minute series) or USGS Libby, Montana (1:100,000-scale metric)

Photo by Jared Douglas

Thad Laird high on the Standard Route on Ojibway Peak

During the summer of 2003, a hiking guidebook called "Trails of the Wild Cabinets," authored by vivacious hiker and good pal Dennis Nicholls, dropped into the lap of the Inland Northwest outdoor community. On its cover was a beautiful, triangular-shaped rock slab hovering above wildflowers near Rock Lake in the Cabinet Mountains Wilderness. Area rock climbers nearly fell out of their chairs when presented with this photo. Consulting the copyright page of the book, they found the peak had a name – Ojibway. Weeks later, Ojibway Peak was being accosted by members of the local Sandpoint climbing community. Several routes were climbed up the mountain's striking Southwest Face – the same face that graces the cover of "Trails of the Wild Cabinets."

The rock on Ojibway Peak is the area's signature rock type: a quartzite blend of some description. Good in-cut edges are the saving feature that makes climbing direct routes on this face possible. The lower face has more suspicious rock than the upper face but is still manageable. The obvious roof system that slashes across the lower face at about one-third height is one of the main challenges of climbing the peak. Thanks in large part to local climbers Vince Regalis and Paul Haraf, a sneaker move up through the left side of the roof has been established to create access to the upper face.

The upper face is spectacular: smooth rock littered with tiny, in-cut edges. The face in general is steep enough to be adventurous but laid back enough to allow for moderate grades up it. Protection is not excellent on Ojibway Peak. Pitons are generally used if climbing direct or new routes on the upper face, especially for the belays. It may be advisable for climbers to carry pitons if attempting The Direct Route or any new routes up the gut of the upper face. However, no pitons are needed on The Standard Route.

The only known fixed anchor on the face is located on Dead Tree Ledge on pitch four of The Standard Route. This anchor is marked by a couple of pitons and a piece of webbing that can be used as a possible emergency bail-off point. Please note that no bolts are allowed on this face as per the U.S. Forest Service ban on bolting in Wilderness Areas. People who place bolts on this face run the risk of having it closed to climbing permanently.

History

In 1966, the dynamic duo of John Roskelley and Chris Kopczynski climbed the broken gully system on the far left side of the face. In more recent years, Roskelley partnered with his son, Jess, and climbed a route up through the left side of the massive roof that splits the lower portion of the face, then continued up a curving crack system that ended about two-thirds of the way up the face on the far right side. This route is reported to be excellent. Beyond that, the history of climbing on Ojibway Peak is a mystery. Perhaps it is up to the next generation of climbers to create that history.

Camping

Despite the fact that Ojibway Peak sits within easy access of the Rock Lake trailhead (and is therefore a viable car-to-car excursion), some may wish to overnight at Rock Lake. This option allows parties to also climb the amazing south ridge of Elephant Peak (IV 5.6) as part of a multiday itinerary. Camping at Rock Lake is best done on the southern side of the lake near its outlet stream. A variety of established sites can be found here. Please note that Rock Lake itself is situated just inside the Cabinet Mountains Wilderness boundary and care should be taken when camping or traveling in this fragile ecosystem.

Amenities

The closest amenities are located in the town of Noxon, Montana, on Highway 200. A small store is located here as well as a small motel. Farther west on Highway 200 is a popular local bar, The Boar's Breath, that serves beer and pub food.

Emergency Facilities

Emergency facilities are located in Sandpoint, Idaho, (roughly 50 miles west of Noxon, Montana, on Highway 200). Alternatively, if you drive north of Noxon on Highway 56 and turn right onto Highway 2 you will reach Libby, Montana, where emergency facilities are located. Driving times are comparable. The closest pay phone is located in Noxon.

Getting There

Two miles east of Noxon, Montana (roughly 50 miles east of Sandpoint, Idaho, and roughly 136 miles northwest of Missoula, Montana), turn north off Highway 200 near milepost 17 onto Rock Creek Road No. 150. After a couple hundred yards, take the right fork and go about six miles to the junction of Road No. 150A. Bear right onto Road No. 150A and follow it 1.5 miles to the trailhead for Rock Lake Trail No. 935.

A) Approach to Ojibway Peak via Rock Lake

Approach

Begin by hiking the well-maintained Rock Lake Trail, which begins as an old road bed. Some may wish to bring mountain bikes for this section, which is steep in spots, but offers a fun, fast and exhilarating descent back to the car at the end of your day. The trail crosses Rock Creek a couple of times and then passes through the old Heidelberg Mine area, where remnants of old cabins and industrial debris can still be seen. The trail then passes through a lovely open area called the Rock Creek Meadows. Just past these meadows, the old road bed enters woods (stash bikes here if using them) and then ends near a waterfall. From here, pick up a brushy, single-track trail that switchbacks for another mile or so up to Rock Lake. The total distance from the car to the lake is about four miles.

From the outlet stream at Rock Lake, hike overland in an easterly manner, aiming for a broad gully system that splits the steep, rocky bluffs below the Southwest Face of Ojibway Peak, which is easily seen high above the eastern shores of the lake. (See photo on previous page for details.) The easiest approach is to scramble up bear grass slopes located just right of the actual gully until it is possible to step left into the gully at about half-height. This technique will avoid some uncomfortable scrambling and brush in the lower portion of the gully. Once you have gained the gully proper, scramble up to its top. Once above the gully, hike up the broad talus field to the base of the Southwest Face.

Routes are described left to right.

WG) West Gully (5th Class)

Not much is known about this dirty gully except that it is dirty and that it was climbed at least once in the 1960s.

V) Variation/Standard Route (5.6) 2 pitches/gear to 2 inches

For parties not comfortable with climbing up through the massive roof system on the Standard Route, an option exists. Uphill, a couple hundred feet from the base of the Standard Route, is a series of shallow, somewhat dirty, left-facing corner systems. They are, at times, unsavory but take climbers all the way up to Dead Tree Ledge, where parties can access the excellent corner system on the fourth pitch of The Standard Route. Once Dead Tree Ledge is gained, proceed up the remainder of The Standard Route.

SR) Standard Route (5.7) 6 to 7 pitches/gear to 4 inches

A fun, somewhat wandering route that begins in the obvious, right-facing, broken corner system just left of center at the bottom of the face. This corner rises to meet the far left side of the major roof system that caps the entire lower face.

Pitch 1: Climb the obvious, right-facing corner (loose in spots) for a full 250 feet. Most parties will want to simul-climb this section rather than try and break it up into two pitches. Belay from a large ledge at the top of the corner.

Pitch 2: The massive roof above and to the right of the ledge is characterized by an obvious weakness. Follow right-slanting slabs and face climb up to the weakness. The crux move through the roof is best protected with a 3.5-inch to 4-inch piece. The rock is down sloping but generally sound. Once through the

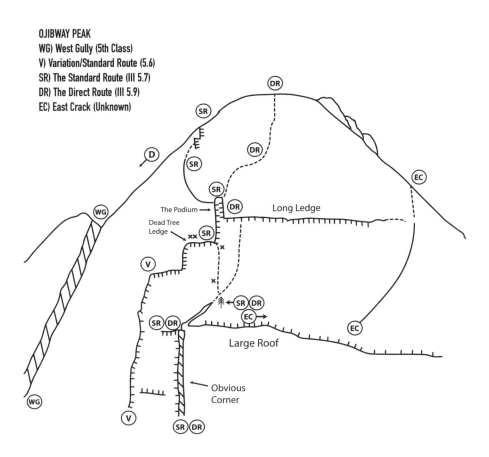

OJIBWAY PEAK
WG) West Gully (5th Class)
V) Variation/Standard Route (5.6)
SR) The Standard Route (III 5.7)
DR) The Direct Route (III 5.9)
EC) East Crack (Unknown)

The Podium →
Dead Tree Ledge →
Long Ledge
Large Roof
Obvious Corner

roof, continue up the right-trending crack system and belay from a small tree.

Pitch 3: This pitch involves leaving the crack system and traversing out left onto the face. From the tree belay, it may be possible to see an old piton on the face above and to the left. Climb up to the piton and then continue directly up the face via in-cut edges and some interesting rock. The goal of this pitch is to gain Dead Tree Ledge, which sits at the base of the obvious, left-facing corner system just left of center on the upper face (aka The Podium). To do this, climb directly up the face until even with, but just right of, Dead Tree Ledge. Clip a second piton here and traverse directly left to Dead Tree Ledge. A fixed anchor has been established on this ledge.

Pitch 4: This exceptional pitch will have every climber wishing it was at least 100 feet longer. Avoid brush at the base of the corner by starting out left and face climbing for roughly 20 feet before moving right into the corner itself. Stem and jam to the top of the corner and belay on a tiny platform known as The Podium. This small ledge is the last portion of flatness before the upper face sets in (the face directly above The Podium is the Direct Route). Anchors can be tricky to find on this ledge, but a rock horn at the lip is often used to aid in the belay process.

The Podium

SR

Amazing corner pitch on the Standard Route on Ojibway Peak

Pitch 5: From The Podium, traverse directly out left beneath the upper face via a narrow ledge system (at times less than 1 foot wide). Excellent views of the south ridge of Elephant Peak can be seen to the north. Traverse this ledge out left until directly below an obvious, somewhat brush-filled, curving crack that rises above the ledge toward the summit area. Proceed up this crack system and belay at a small, dead tree. (Note: It is generally best to climb in-cut

Paul Haraf on the first known ascent of The Direct Route on Ojibway Peak

edges on the face just right of the actual crack system.)

Pitch 6: Continue up the curving crack system, alternating between face climbing on the right side of the crack and climbing the crack itself. Vegetation will dictate which method is best. Aim for a series of short corners and flakes directly above the curving crack. Belay on a small pedestal just below these corners.

Pitch 7: Climb a short corner system to the summit ridge. Belay on the ridge crest. From here, most parties will opt to unrope and scramble the remainder of the fourth-class North Ridge to the summit area. (Note: It is hard to tell which clump of rocks are the true summit of Ojibway Peak. But a high point with a small cairn set a few hundred yards back from the top of the Southwest Face is commonly referred to as "the summit.")

Descent: Scramble down the North Ridge until it is possible to drop off the west side of the ridge and curve back under the Southwest Face. A few short, steep sections on the North Ridge may require spotting or perhaps even minor rope work, for some parties.

DR) Direct Route (5.9) 6 pitches/gear to 4 inches plus pitons

This exceptional direct route begins as for The Standard Route in the obvious, broken corner system just left of center at the bottom of the face. Instead of moving up and left to Dead Tree Ledge, however, the route gains The Podium from its right-hand side and then climbs directly above The Podium (trending right) up the gut of the upper face.

Pitch 1: Climb the obvious, broken right-facing corner (loose in spots) for a full 250 feet. Most parties will want to simul-climb this section rather than try to break it up into two pitches. Belay from a large ledge at the top of the corner.

Pitch 2: The massive roof above and to the right of the ledge is characterized by an obvious weakness. Follow right-slanting slabs and face climb up to the weakness. The crux move through the roof is best protected with a 3.5-inch to 4-inch piece. The rock is down sloping but generally sound. Once through the roof, continue up the right-trending crack system and belay from a small tree.

Pitch 3: Climb the face directly above the tree belay, which ends at a long ledge that divides the upper face. Move left and belay at the short, shallow, right-facing corner that makes up the right-hand side of The Podium.

Pitches 4 and 5: Lieback the shallow, right-facing corner up to The Podium. The remainder of the route climbs the smooth face above via challenging route-finding and thin gear placements. This is where the knife-blade pitons may come in handy. The face appears unclimbable at first but is endowed with a variety of in-cut edges. The crux is a short, right-trending traverse over loose blocks. Many parties will find pitons useful for the belays as well. Belay in the middle of the face after passing through several loose blocks.

Pitch 6: A brilliant position on this exposed face, this pitch punches directly up the gut of the face to the top. The route ends a few feet shy of the summit cairns with beautiful summit views of all the other adventures that await in the Cabinet Mountains Wilderness.

Descent: As for The Standard Route via the North Ridge.

EC) East Crack (Unknown)

Not much is known about this route, except that it surmounts an obvious weakness on the left side of the massive roof, follows a curving crack for a couple of pitches and then ends on the far right side of the Southwest Face below the summit area. Scramble up to the summit and descend the North Ridge.

Elephant Peak

Elephant Peak (7,938 feet)

Number of Routes: One known

Grade: IV 5.6

Length: 10+ pitches (if entire route is belayed)

Approach Time: 5 hours

Climbing Time: 4 to 6 hours

Total Elevation Gain (car to summit): 4,734 feet

Descent Type: Walk-off

Season: Generally June through late September

Maps: USGS Elephant Peak (7.5-minute series) or USGS Libby, Montana (1:100,000-scale metric)

The South Ridge of Elephant Peak is a long, fantastic, high ridge route in the Cabinet Mountains Wilderness. It is highly recommended for strong teams who are willing to move fast over exposed terrain. If you opt to belay every pitch, this route is probably about 15 pitches long. Simul-climbing is the recommended method on this route. The ridge can be seen from the Southwest Face of Ojibway Peak, as well as from the St. Paul Peak/Rock Peak saddle, which is encountered on the approach to St. Paul Peak via Cliff Lake.

During an ascent of the peak in 2003, a few old pitons were encountered on the route, all of which were located on the steep gendarmes/walls that break up the ridge. Numerous variations and bail-off spots exist along this route. Please note that it can be done as a long car-to-car day from the Rock Lake trailhead (12 to 14 hours) roundtrip. However, most parties should opt to overnight at Rock Lake. If this is the chosen method, it is recommended that you add a day to your itinerary to tackle the Southwest Face of Ojibway Peak, which sits directly above Rock Lake.

Camping
Overnight camping is best done at Rock Lake. There are a handful of primitive sites located at the southern end of the lake near the outlet stream. Please note that Rock Lake is situated just inside the Cabinet Mountains Wilderness boundary. Care should be taken when camping in this fragile ecosystem.

Amenities
The closest amenities are located in the town of Noxon, Montana, on Highway 200. A small store is located here as well as a small motel. Farther west on Highway 200 is a popular local bar, The Boar's Breath, that serves beer and pub food.

Emergency Facilities
Emergency facilities are located in Sandpoint, Idaho, (roughly 50 miles west of Noxon, Montana, on Highway 200). Alternatively, if you drive north of Noxon

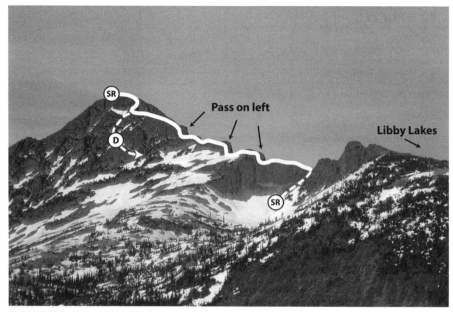

ELEPHANT PEAK SR) South Ridge (IV 5.6) 10-plus pitches D) Descent (Walk-Off)

on Highway 56 and turn right onto Highway 2, you will reach Libby, Montana, where emergency facilities are located. Driving times are comparable. The closest pay phone is located in Noxon.

Getting There

Two miles east of Noxon, Montana (roughly 50 miles east of Sandpoint, Idaho, and 136 miles northwest of Missoula, Montana) turn north off Highway 200 near milepost 17 onto Rock Creek Road No. 150. After a couple hundred yards, take the right fork and go about six miles to the junction of Road No. 150A. Bear right onto Road No. 150A and follow it 1.5 miles to the trailhead for Rock Lake Trail No. 935.

Approach

Begin by hiking the well-maintained Rock Lake Trail, which begins as an old mining road. Some may wish to bring mountain bikes for this section, which is steep in spots, but offers a fun, fast and exhilarating descent back to the car at the end of your day. The trail crosses Rock Creek a couple of times and then passes through the old Heidelberg Mine area, where remnants of old cabins and industrial debris can still be seen. The trail then passes through a lovely open area called the Rock Creek meadows. Just past these meadows, the old road bed enters woods (stash bikes here if using them) and then ends near a waterfall. From here, pick up a brushy single track trail that switchbacks for another mile or so up to Rock Lake. The total distance from the car to the lake is about four miles.

The remainder of the approach into Elephant Peak is quite long and tricky. It is highly recommended that one follow the USGS Elephant Peak topographical map very closely, and remember that the peak itself is not actually seen until well into the approach, high above Libby Lakes.

From Rock Lake, hike around the left (west) side of the lake using existing trails. Once you reach the inlet stream that feeds Rock Lake, it is advisable to use the actual streambed as the approach. Dennis Nicholls' authoritative book on hiking in the Cabinets called "Trails of the Wild Cabinets" (Keokee Publishing, 2003) describes a trail system which leads north from here. However, having bushwhacked for hours through this region, no such trail was found, which doesn't mean one isn't there; it just means I was probably having a bad day. Again, it may be best to get your boots wet by scrambling up the inlet stream. Be aware, the rocks are slippery. After sorting through the creek bed for about 45 minutes, start looking up to your right (east) and locate a long grassy slope rising steeply above you. On the USGS Elephant Peak map, this slope appears to lead to the Libby Lakes, which it does. These gorgeous, high-mountain lakes are your first major goal on the approach.

Once at the northernmost lake of the Libby Lake group, proceed up and over a small pass to the north. At the top of this pass, you get your first real views of Elephant Peak. Drop off the north side of the pass and hike below some high rocky crags that are directly east of you. These are sub-peaks and satellite peaks that don't deserve your attention.

The next goal is to locate a major gully system on the west side of the south ridge (located due north of the aforementioned sub-peaks). This gully is scrambled up to the crest of the south ridge. Rope up here.

SR) South Ridge (5.6) 10-plus pitches/gear to 2.5 inches

The route essentially follows the ridge crest for many rope lengths, passing all obstacles in the form of large gendarmes/walls on the left (west) via face climbing. A few pitons will be encountered along the way. Near the end of the ridge, it makes a dramatic dogleg to the east and becomes The East Ridge. This spur ridge gains talus fields just south of the main summit area.

Descent: From the summit area, follow gully systems down the west side of the peak. The goal is to end up below The South Ridge on its west side. Hike bear grass and talus slopes back to the pass above upper Libby Lake. Retrace your steps back down to Rock Lake.

St. Paul Peak

St. Paul Peak (7,714 feet)

Number of Routes: Three known

Grade Range: 5.7 to 5.10 (Plus snow routes to 55 degrees)

Length Range: 8 to 10 pitches

Vertical Gain (Car to Summit): 1,314 feet

Approach Time: 2 hours via Cliff Lake; 4 hours via St. Paul Lake

Climbing Time: 4 to 8 hours

Descent Type: Walk-off

Season: May through September

Maps: USGS Elephant Peak (7.5-minute series) or USGS Libby, Montana (1:100,000-scale metric)

St. Paul Peak is a broad, bulky mountain with dramatic rock faces tumbling off its north and east sides. The peak sits northwest of the Rock Lake area and just east of the Bull River Valley (i.e. the Highway 56 corridor). The mountain's awesome East Face can be seen from St. Paul Lake, which sits northeast of the peak. Its gentle southeastern aspects join with nearby Rock Peak's northwest ridge to create the St. Paul Peak/Rock Peak saddle near Cliff Lake.

St. Paul's proximity to the popular hiking destination of Cliff Lake, coupled with its gentle southern aspects, makes this peak an easy destination for hikers. Rock climbers also benefit from the peak's proximity to Cliff Lake by having a relatively short approach and one of the easiest descents in the Cabinet Range. Backcountry skiers will also find this area to be an excellent spring destination.

St. Paul Peak is endowed with a rock type highly favored by rock climbers: a quartzite blend. This smooth, grayish-red, picturesque rock type is characterized by positive in-cut edges. Indeed, seemingly unclimbable sections of St. Paul Peak's faces can often be surmounted via these tiny in-cut handholds. On the flip side, it is important to know that sedimentary rock faces often form in large steps. This phenomenon is clearly evident in Glacier National Park to the east and the Canadian Rockies to the north. The Northeast Arête (III 5.7+) on St. Paul Peak is a classic example of this geological condition. The route is characterized by large steps of rock where technical climbing can be found, followed by treed ledges that disrupt the rock climbing but provide excellent belay platforms. The most redeeming factor of St. Paul Peak is the grandeur and exposure that overcomes the climber the higher one climbs. At roughly 1,200 feet in vertical height, the East Face, Northeast Arête and Number Seven Gully offer a big mountain experience in a pristine setting, all within easy access of the road. This said, it would be unwise to underestimate the size of this peak. Some climbers may find it to be a very adventurous undertaking. All climbers will find it to be beautiful and unique – drenched in that certain sense of isolation found in the Cabinet Mountains Wilderness.

History

Decades ago, John Roskelley pushed a route up the gut of the East Face. In an e-mail Roskelley wrote to the author, he said that the route "was just right of the major cleft in the center of the face and included several long lead outs over difficult terrain." No further information is available about this route.

As for the Northeast Arête, extensive archeological digging was performed on two different ascents of the route, one in 2003 and the other in 2005, both completed by the author and Bill Kish. No evidence of previous ascents of the Northeast Arête was found. As for the Number Seven Gully, no evidence of any nature was found on this route either. However, given that it is a snow route and is subject to seasonal melting, it seems doubtful that any evidence would have existed in the first place. It is unknown whether these lines were climbed prior to 2003. It is hoped that further information on these climbing routes will surface over time.

Camping

Car camping at the Cliff Lake trailhead is the preferred method for staging assaults on St. Paul Peak, if approaching via Cliff Lake. However, camping at Cliff Lake itself is possible at primitive sites. It is also possible to bivouac at the St. Paul-Rock Peak saddle. Water may be a concern if camping at the saddle in late summer. If using the alternative Bull River Approach, camping is best done at St. Paul Lake.

Amenities

The closest amenities are located in the town of Noxon, Montana, on Highway 200. A small store is located here as well as a small motel. Farther west on Highway 200 is a popular local bar, The Boar's Breath, that serves beer and pub food.

Emergency Facilities

Emergency facilities are located in Sandpoint, Idaho, (roughly 50 miles west of Noxon, Montana, on Highway 200). Alternatively, if you drive north of Noxon on Highway 56 and turn right onto Highway 2, you will reach Libby, Montana, where emergency facilities are located. Driving times are comparable. The closest pay phone is located in Noxon.

Getting There (Cliff Lake Approach)

The standard (and easiest) approach into St. Paul Peak is via Cliff Lake. However, this approach requires either a high-clearance vehicle or a particular need to destroy a low-clearance one. If vehicles permit, drive two miles east of Noxon, Montana (which is roughly 50 miles east of Sandpoint, Idaho, and roughly 136 miles northwest of Missoula, Montana), turn north off Highway 200 near milepost 17 onto Rock Creek Road No. 150. After a couple hundred yards, take the right fork and follow Road No. 150 for about eight miles to Chicago Peak Road No. 2741. Turn right onto this road, which climbs nearly 2,600 feet following narrow, rocky terrain and numerous switchbacks. A few side roads veer off the main road but lead to dead ends. The road ends at the trailhead.

Author's Note: It is possible to drive a majority of this road with no clearance issues, and park when clearance (or snow) dictates. This would simply add about three extra miles of road hiking onto the approach. If vehicle clearance or snowpack are issues, please follow the alternative Bull River Approach. This is a much longer approach but provides a viable alternative for reaching this amazing peak.

Standard (Cliff Lake) Approach

From the Cliff Lake trailhead, follow the well-maintained trail about 1.5 miles to the lake. This is a quick, easy, lovely walk through subalpine terrain. The next goal is to gain the St. Paul Peak-Rock Peak saddle located roughly a half mile east of Cliff Lake. To do this, hike around the southern edge of the lake, cross its outlet stream, and gain the small wooded slope directly above. From here, use existing game trails and bear grass slopes to traverse directly east, aiming for the broad saddle between St. Paul Peak and Rock Peak. While there is some up-and-down hiking on this portion of the approach, the elevation difference between Cliff Lake and the saddle is only about 100 feet.

Once you gain the St. Paul Peak-Rock Peak saddle, look off the saddle's east side and notice the steep drop below. Your next objective is to rappel off the saddle into the basin to the east. It is best to stash packs or extra food, gear, dogs, non-climber girlfriends or boyfriends, etc., at the saddle before rappelling. You will be descending from the summit of St. Paul Peak to this exact spot after the climb. On a side note, the south ridge of Elephant Peak (IV 5.6) can be seen

St. Paul Approach via Cliff Lake, photo taken after rappelling from saddle

in profile directly across the valley to the east.

After rappelling off the St. Paul Peak-Rock Peak saddle, hike north below the mountain's East Face. If the East Face is your objective, locate the obvious cleft in the center of the face. The old Roskelley route charges up the right side of this cleft via wide cracks and face climbing. No further information is known about this route.

If your objective is the Northeast Arête or the Number Seven Gully, continue walking below the East Face, aiming for the toe of the buttress that tumbles off the mountain's northeast side. At the toe of the buttress, notice an S-shaped syncline formation in the rock. Directly below this swirling formation is a ledge system. Gain this ledge and move out right for about 30 feet until you see a steep gully/weakness directly above. Scramble up this weakness (fourth class at times) for about 50 feet, then bear right and continue up another grassy gully that eventually leads to the base of the Northeast Arête. The best way to know that you have found the base of the route is to locate a small rock tower (perhaps 40 feet high) called "The Pinky." The Pinky is nearly impossible to see on the earlier portion of the approach, but once you gain the slopes directly below the Northeast Arête, The Pinky becomes very obvious sitting at the bottom of the Number Seven Gully.

Alternative Bull River Approach

If you encounter vehicle-clearance issues on the Standard Cliff Lake Approach, it is possible to approach via St. Paul Lake and gain the East Face, Northeast Arête and Number Seven Gully from there.

ST. PAUL PEAK (photo taken from St. Paul Lake)
EF) East Face (Unknown)
NE) Northeast Arête (III 5.7+) 8 to 10 pitches
NS) The Number Seven Gully (III 5.5/Snow to 55+ degrees)
V) Variation

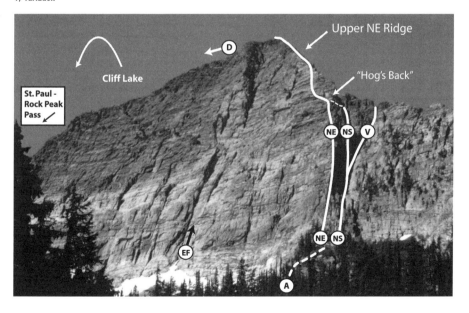

From Noxon, Montana, turn north onto Highway 56 (the Bull River Highway) and proceed about 13 miles. Turn right (east) onto Road No. 407 (at the eight mile marker) and proceed six miles to the St. Paul Lake Trail No. 646 trailhead.

Hike the well-maintained trail for about four miles into St. Paul Lake. The dramatic eastern aspects of St. Paul Peak are reflected in the lake; its glowing rock walls beckon climbers to it. From the south end of the lake, travel overland through a gully/valley system located above the shores of the lake, which leads in the general direction of the peak. Some heavy brush may be encountered in this gully/valley. The name of the game is to persevere until you break out of the brush and enter the large basin below the East Face of St. Paul Peak. Here, lovely rock slabs and cascades offer a fine place to rest before choosing your line of ascension and method of attack. To descend from the summit, walk down the southern slopes of the peak (as for the standard descent route), rappel off the east side of the St. Paul Peak-Rock Peak saddle into the basin and follow the gully/valley back down to St. Paul Lake. This approach takes about three to four hours, which is considerably longer than the Cliff Lake approach, but well worth it if it's your only choice. An overnight spent at St. Paul Lake would break up the trip nicely. However, a car-to-car blitz is still viable via this approach.

EF) East Face (Unknown)

This route is said to climb the right side of the major cleft in the center of the face. No further information is available about this route.

NE) Northeast Arête (5.7+) 8 to 10 pitches/gear to 3 inches

Pitch 1: The start of the route is characterized by a large block with a crack, located just left of a wide corner system. Jam the crack, using good face holds on either side. Near the top of the pitch, bear right, stepping across the wide crack and finishing at trees on a large ledge. (80 feet/5.5)

Pitch 2: Several variations exist on this pitch. 1) Climb the fin above via fun but dirty cracks and edges. 2) Skirt the fin on the right via a gully that leads to a short, cruxy corner. 3) Skirt the fin on the left via slabs and some brush. Either way, belay from trees near the crest of the arête, which is marked by a clean, gray slab with a piton about 15 feet up it. (140 feet/5.5-5.7)

Pitch 3: This is the money pitch. Climb up to the piton via fun face moves on good in-cut edges. Clip the piton and continue directly up and out right toward a small roof system. Look for a thin crack for pro below the roof, then move directly out right to the crest of the arête. Climb up through the right side of the roof pinching the arête itself with your right hand. Pull through the roof, passing a second piton, and continue up a short, blocky section to a ledge with dead trees. (120 feet/5.7+)

Pitch 4: Climb directly up and over the blocky rib located near the crest of the arête. Once past the blocky rib, trend up and right through trees, aiming for the ridge crest. A small step leads to a treed ledge. (140 feet/5th class)

Pitch 5: By far the least aesthetic or interesting pitch on the climb, this section is characterized by lots of trees and some suspicious rock. Begin on a short, clean slab left of center and enter the trees. Head for a V-shaped notch in the horizon and pull past it up to the Hog's Back – a rib of rock that juts out at a

Bill Kish climbs the upper Northeast Ridge. St. Paul Lake is seen in the background.

perpendicular angle to the arête. (Note: Peer off the back side of The Hog's Back and notice a steep gully with steep rock walls on either side. This is the upper portion of the Number Seven Gully). (200+ feet/5th class)

Pitch 6: Hike up and left via grassy slopes to a high point at the base of the obvious headwall. (100 feet/3rd class)

Pitches 7 and 8: Climb directly up the headwall on good, down-sloping quartzite. A short, steep wall about 50 feet up is best passed on the left. Continue picking your way over interesting terrain for several long rope lengths (simul-climbing is recommended here) until you gain the crest of the upper Northeast Ridge, which leads directly to the summit. (400+ feet/5.5)

Upper Pitches: Most parties will elect to unrope once they have gained the upper Northeast Ridge and scramble the remainder of the route to the top. Stay directly on the crest for the best climbing. A few obstacles on the ridge are generally passed on the left. (400+ feet/4th class)

Descent: From the summit area, hike south via bear grass slopes and a few patches of trees. Return to the St. Paul-Rock Peak saddle, collect your things, and follow your footsteps back the way you came in. In high summer, a brisk dip into Cliff Lake puts the true glory of this climbing life into perspective.

NS) Number Seven Gully (5.5/Snow to 55+ degrees) Simul-climbing plus 3 to 4 roped pitches/gear to 1.5 inches plus snow pickets

Approach as for the Northeast Arête. From The Pinky formation located near the base of that route, the obvious gully directly above is the beginning of The Number Seven Gully.

This excellent snow couloir offers one of the finest alpine climbing experiences in this entire guide-book. It was stumbled upon during an ascent of the Northeast Arête. The upper portion of the gully is characterized by a dramatic leftward dogleg (thus named the Number Seven Gully) which is easily missed if the climber is not paying attention. A thin snow finger (up to 60 degrees depending on conditions) leads up this dogleg and ends at the base of the headwall encountered on the upper Northeast Arête route. Experienced parties will not need to carry much extra rock gear, such as rock shoes or an extensive rack. The upper headwall pitches can be climbed in leather boots (5.5 at the most) with a small rack of nuts, slings and maybe a couple of small cams for insurance. If this gully were in the Cascades, it would surely be a Fred Beckey

Paul Haraf climbs The Number Seven Gully.

route written up in all the "Select Classics" books. Then again, there's always a chance that it is a Fred Beckey route that has simply been lost to the ages.

Begin by climbing third-/fourth-class rock (or snow) inside the lower gully. Eventually the gully narrows into an excellent snow couloir. After a few hundred feet, begin looking out left for a thin sneaker gully (dogleg) which branches out of the main gully. This dramatic dogleg is easily missed if you get too caught up in the pleasant climbing. Follow this dogleg, which immediately steepens and contains vertical rock walls on either side. This excellent snow finger tops out at the Hog's Back, which is situated at the base of the upper headwall on the Northeast Arête. Finish as for the remainder of the Northeast Arête via mid-fifth-class rock climbing.

V) Variation (Snow to 45 degrees)

If you continue climbing the main gully system and do not opt for the dramatic, leftward dogleg on the Number Seven Gully, you will end up in a basin directly north of the summit area. From here it is possible to climb steep snow slopes to the summit.

Descent: As for the Northeast Arête.

Snowshoe Peak

Snowshoe Peak (8,738 feet)

Number of Routes: One known scramble; all others are hikes

Grade: 3rd to 4th class

Length: Roughly 1 mile of ridge scrambling

Approach Time: 3 hours

Climbing Time: 3 hours

Total Elevation Gain (car to summit): 4,538 feet

Descent Type: Walk-off

Season: Generally June through late September

Maps: USGS Snowshoe Peak (7.5-minute series) or USGS Libby, Montana (1:100,000-scale metric)

Thad Laird scrambles on the Northeast Spur of Snowshoe Peak.

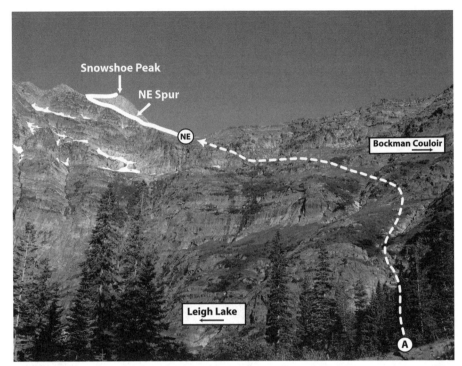

SNOWSHOE PEAK
A) Approach via Leigh Lake
NE) Northeast Spur (3rd/4th Class)

Snowshoe Peak is the tallest peak in the Cabinet Range and dominates the horizon when viewed from many high points along the Selkirk Crest. Snowshoe's broad, bulky shape instantly brings to mind the high peaks of the Rocky Mountains. The entire Snowshoe Massif, which includes A Peak to its north and Bockman Peak to its northeast, offers a fabulous destination for the mountain enthusiast.

When viewed from the west (along Highway 56 in the Bull River Valley), Snowshoe Peak offers few visual clues that are of interest to climbers. These western slopes are a popular destination for ski mountaineers and summer hikers. From the east, however, the lofty cirques and headwalls overlooking Leigh Lake are spectacular in terms of climbing potential. Rumors of mixed ice routes above Leigh Lake (aka The Leigh Lake Cirque) have been passed through the local climbing community for years. No further information on their validity has been confirmed.

The Northeast Spur route on Snowshoe Peak is a historic route that some consider the greatest mountain scramble in the entire Cabinet Mountains Wilderness. The route is not very technical but is long, exposed in spots and is undoubtedly strenuous. Any way you slice it, this route is a very rewarding day spent in a beautiful mountain landscape.

One of the most unique portions of the scramble is its crossing of the upper Blackwell Glacier. The Blackwell Glacier rises up from the Granite Lake basin located directly north of Snowshoe Peak and ends at a tall chunk of rock known as the Blackwell Headwall just below the summit area. This steep headwall of fractured rock would make an interesting, if not frightening, climb. Rumors that Fred Beckey put a route up on it in the 1960s have never been confirmed. The Northeast Spur route crosses the Blackwell Glacier near the base of the headwall, skirts all major rock obstacles by curving south and then gains the final ridge to the summit. As would be expected, views from the summit of Snowshoe Peak are vast, allowing the climber to get a glimpse of the true grandness of the Cabinet Mountains Wilderness.

Camping
Many parties will opt to car camp at the Leigh Lake trailhead and do the Northeast Spur route as a marathon day. However, backcountry camping on the northeast side of Leigh Lake is a viable option. Please remember that you will be camping within the boundaries of the Cabinet Mountains Wilderness. Take special care to leave no trace.

Amenities
The closest amenities are located in the town of Libby, Montana, located on Highway 2. The town is small, but it has many restaurants, bars and motels.

Emergency Facilities
The closest emergency facilities, as well as the nearest pay phone, are located in the town of Libby, Montana, on Highway 2.

NE) Northeast Spur (3rd/4th Class)
?) Possible climbing routes

Getting There

Approximately eight miles east of Libby, Montana, turn right (southwest) off Highway 2 onto Big Cherry Creek Road No. 278. After three miles, turn west onto Road No. 867 and proceed five miles to the junction of Road No. 4786. Follow this road about two miles to the trailhead for Leigh Lake Trail No. 132.

Approach

From the Leigh Lake trailhead, follow the steep trail for about 1.5 miles to the lake. Follow the brushy northern edges of the lake (best trails are located near the lakeshore), aiming for the steep grassy slopes located directly north of the lake. It is best to find a broad couloir that tumbles down off Bockman Peak into the lake. This deep, dramatic couloir is an excellent backcountry ski trip in early spring.

Proceed up the couloir until it is possible to begin bearing up and left (west) toward the high ridge above. This high ridge runs between Bockman Peak and Snowshoe Peak, and is your first major goal on the approach. Traveling up through the steep grassy slopes north of Leigh Lake to the ridge is essentially a free-for-all. Simply choose the path of least resistance. Review the Approach Photo (provided in this section) for an idea of how to pick a route to the high ridge.

Once on the high ridge between Bockman Peak and Snowshoe Peak, look westward toward Snowshoe Peak and review the terrain. The ridge you are on begins as a broad, brush-covered mountain feature but slowly steepens as it rises to meet the upper flanks of the Snowshoe Headwall. The rocky portion of the ridge crest in front of you is the Northeast Spur.

NE) Northeast Spur (3rd/4th Class) A non-technical climb for most parties

Scramble up the obvious spur ridge, staying as close to the crest as possible. A few small obstacles in the form of gullies or short walls can be passed easily on the left (south) or climbed directly for added fun. The ridge is generally not technical, or too terribly steep, but offers exciting scrambling opportunities high above the Leigh Lake Cirque and the Granite Lake Basin.

At about the 8,000-foot level, the ridge becomes gentler. Here, the upper reaches of the Blackwell Glacier rise up to join the Northeast Spur below the looming Blackwell Headwall. Hike up the left edge of the glacier/snowfield (no crampons needed) until it is possible to curve south around to the south ridge of Snowshoe Peak. From this point, gain the summit ridge and proceed up through funky rock formations and slabs to the top.

Descent: Retrace your steps down to Leigh Lake, take a quick dip in its brisk waters and then go drink beer in Libby.

Cresting the Northeast Spur with the Blackwell Glacier in the background. Granite Creek lies beyond.

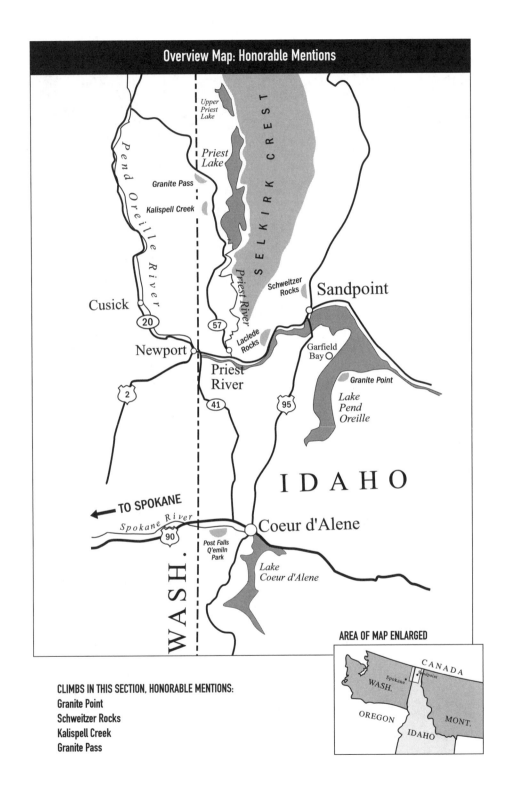

Overview Map: Honorable Mentions

Upper Priest Lake

Priest Lake

Granite Pass

Kalispell Creek

Pend Oreille River

SELKIRK CREST

Priest River

Schweitzer Rocks

Sandpoint

Cusick

20

57

Laclede Rocks

Newport

Garfield Bay

Priest River

Granite Point

2

41

95

Lake Pend Oreille

IDAHO

TO SPOKANE

Spokane River

90

Coeur d'Alene

Post Falls Q'emiln Park

WASH.

Lake Coeur d'Alene

AREA OF MAP ENLARGED

CANADA

WASH.

Spokane

Sandpoint

OREGON

MONT.

IDAHO

CLIMBS IN THIS SECTION, HONORABLE MENTIONS:
Granite Point
Schweitzer Rocks
Kalispell Creek
Granite Pass

Section IV:

Honorable Mentions

As with any climbing region, some crags are either rarely visited or too new for a guidebook author to make any real judgments about. The following list of climbs makes brief mention of bits of rock that may be of interest to motivated rock climbers. These crags are worth checking out as long as the climber realizes that they need to be approached with an open mind, an adventurous spirit and perhaps even a few scrub brushes.

Granite Point, Lake Pend Oreille (North Idaho)

In the early 1980s, the Granite Point Crags, which are located at the feet of the Green Monarch Mountains on the eastern shores of Lake Pend Oreille, were a hot spot of climbing activity. Randall Green and company made numerous trips to the region and established bold, exhilarating free climbs high above the lake. As the years passed and a new generation of climbers moved into the area, Granite Point saw far less traffic. As a result, the dreaded "black lettuce" munge associated with long North Idaho winters crept back onto the cliff faces, hardware began to rust and a few important blocks gave way to the powers of erosion.

Today, Granite Point is still remote and beautiful but is in serious need of a face-lift. An attempt at such a face-lift in the summer of 2005 was thwarted by unseasonably bad climbing conditions and a desire to fix Laclede's resurrection needs prior to any other area's. However, a handful of expeditions were made to these crags by area climbers who found the routes still to be enjoyable, if not slightly dirty.

Randall Green has kindly allowed the following list of climbs to be reused from his 1987 book, "Idaho Rock." However, please note that some of the climbs may have changed over the years. Climbers looking to explore this area should go there with an adventurous attitude toward climbing and solid lake navigation skills.

Getting There
(via motorboat, kayak, canoe or a very long swim)

Access to these lakeside crags is best via watercraft. The standard launching point is at Garfield Bay located on the Sagle Peninsula near Sandpoint, Idaho. From Sandpoint, take Highway 95 south approximately six miles, turn east onto Sagle Road and follow this 7.2 miles to Garfield Bay Road/Sagle Road junction. Veer right onto Garfield Bay Road and go 1.4 miles to the Garfield Bay boat launch and picnic area.

Directly across the lake (roughly six miles) from the Garfield Bay public boat launch lie the cliffs of Granite Point. It is best to consult the USGS Sandpoint

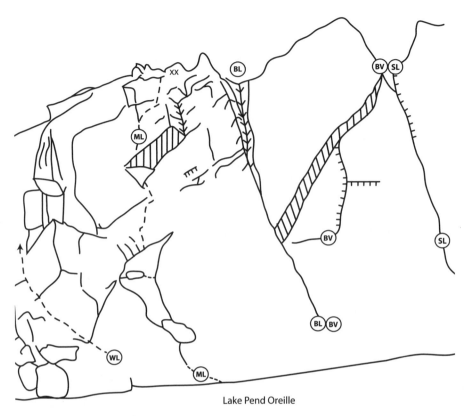

Lake Pend Oreille

GRANITE POINT
WL) Waterline (5.8)
ML) Mainline (5.10d)
BE) Beeline (5.5)
BV) Beeline – 110 Degrees Variation (5.10a)
SL) Shoreline (5.7)

(1:100,000-scale metric) map prior to embarking on this approach. Once you arrive at the crags, many of the climbs are accessed directly from your boat. As a result, it is recommended to bring bumpers or some type of padding to protect your boat from the rocks once you have anchored yourself to them. No permanent moorings exist, so it may be best to use a few nuts or cams and a length of old climbing rope to tie into the rock.

Flying Squirrel Buttress

On the far left side of the waterside crags is a wall characterized by big, white blocks and roofs. This area is called The Flying Squirrel Buttress and holds several fine climbs. Access is directly out of your boat. It is advised to position your boat as far off to one side so as to avoid knocking loose rocks onto it.

WL) Waterline (5.8) Gear to 3 inches/rappel off the Mainline anchors

On the far left side of the crag, at water level, are two square, flat-topped blocks. Waterline starts at these blocks and follows a left-sloping crack past a large block and then continues a short distance above to an obvious belay ledge. Scramble up easy blocks and slabs to the top.

ML) Mainline (5.10d) Fixed gear, plus gear to 2 inches/bolt anchor

Directly in the center of the cliff and to the right of Waterline is a series of blocky roofs. Mainline climbs up through these roofs via cracks and some fixed gear. Face climb up from the water's edge to a flake system, which gives access to a series of overhanging blocks. Climb through the blocks via good, thin cracks (1.5 inches) to the top. A fixed rappel station is located on the top of this climb.

BE) Beeline (5.5) Gear/natural anchor

To the right of Mainline is a left-sloping ramp. Beeline follows this line to the top of the cliff. Ascend a left-sloping crack system past easy ledges to a large pine tree at the top.

BV) Beeline – 110 Degrees Variation (5.10a) Gear/natural anchor

This climb follows a connecting crack system partway up Beeline that connects with Shoreline. Follow Beeline up to a bush until it is possible to move out right and ascend a steep, clean, right-trending crack up to the top of Shoreline.

SL) Shoreline (5.7) Gear/natural anchor

On the far right side of the cliff is a moderate climb that ascends a broken line of cracks and blocks to a prominent notch on the top. Scramble up the bank to a slightly left-sloping crack. Continue up to the notch and stem and jam past steep blocks to the top.

Descent: The best descent is via the fixed anchor on top of Mainline. It is a 90-foot rappel from this anchor system down to the water's edge.

Foreboding Buttress

Fear and Loathing (5.8) (Not shown) 3 pitches Gear/bolt anchor

Along the lakeshore south of The Flying Squirrel Buttress is another waterside wall. Just past this wall is a small cove. Land here and hike uphill toward the walls above. The first large chunk of rock is called Foreboding Buttress and there is one three-pitch climb on it that follows cracks and a few loose sections. Rappel the route with double ropes.

Sunset Buttress

Uphill from the Foreboding Buttress is a large wall with a few obvious crack lines on its face.

Fingerling (5.10c) (Not shown) Gear/bolt anchor

In the middle of the face is a fractured area with two parallel cracks ascending from a large broken alcove. The thin crack on the left is an old aid route (free climb anyone?). The route on the right is a classic 5.10 finger crack called Fingerling. Rappel the route.

(Note: A few routes are located just right of and uphill from Fingerling but seem to have been lost over the years to obscurity.)

Schweitzer Rocks

It hurts me to speak of the Schweitzer Practice Rocks in the past tense, especially when writing a rock climbing guidebook for North Idaho. But the reality of the situation is that Sandpoint is a growing community. And with this influx of people comes the need to build new homes. The housing development of Granite Ridge (located off Granite Ridge Road near the bottom parking lot/bus stop for Schweitzer Mountain) has, unfortunately, blocked access to many of the historic rock climbs there.

In the summer of 2002, a metal gate was erected on the crag's access road and several "No Trespassing" signs began peppering resident pine trees in the area. Then, in the spring of 2003, an area of trees that once provided shade and wind protection on the Upper Main Wall (near Fern Crack) was bulldozed to make room for a homesite. It is apparent that many new homes are slotted for construction in and around the various bluffs and crags that once made up the Schweitzer Practice Rocks.

This said, access to these crags is done entirely at one's risk. The only possible (and by possible I mean, "You are trespassing here, so tread lightly folks!!") exceptions are a few excellent boulders scattered in the woods near the previously mentioned locked metal gate. Also, walking 100 yards past the locked gate leads to a roadside slab with an excellent 5.9 bolted route on it that continues to see ascents. Above the left edge of the slab is another cliff set back in the trees. The farthest left portion of the crag (with the large overhang) has a stout mixed route (several bolts plus gear to 2 inches with a few smaller cams) called "Mosstafarian" (5.10d) that is excellent. The cliff has a couple of pairs of top rope anchors on it. All the other cliffs located high above this slab have (or had) other routes on them. Home building will dictate which ones are lost forever.

Kalispell Creek

Kalispell Creek is an interesting and promising area – a direct result of local climber Tim Chamberlain's quest to establish more rock climbs in North Idaho. An early hike into the area found several superb climbs. Unfortunately, weather did not allow a sampling of the goods. The following are general directions on how to get to the area. According to Tim, many of the climbs are in the 5.11 to 5.12 realm. However, the farthest left climb located on the approach ledge is reported to be 5.9.

Getting There

From the town of Priest River, Idaho, drive north on Highway 57 for approximately 34 miles. Turn left (west) onto Kalispell Creek Road and after about a half mile, notice an overgrown Forest Service road with a gate on your left. Park at the gate.

Approach

Hike the old Forest Service road until you come to an old rock quarry. Hike around the right side of the quarry via a thin trail and enter woods behind the quarry. A climber's trail is picked up here and followed to a large boulder field at the base of the cliffs. Hike up the left side of the boulder field until you reach a broad ledge partway up. This ledge leads to several of the bolted climbs on the face above. All routes are rappelled with double ropes.

Granite Pass ▬ ▬ ▬ ▬ ▬ ▬ ▬ ▬ ▬ ▬

This interesting up-and-coming venue is located roadside in a beautiful valley in a remote location northwest of Priest Lake. A few high-quality sport and gear routes are located here and demand further exploration. The only drawback to these climbs is that they are a long day trip from both the Spokane and Sandpoint areas. However, the crag's relative proximity to Chimney Rock and The Lion's Head makes it a great side trip if doing climbs in the area.

On a sunny afternoon in mid-July, the author climbed a few routes at Chimney Rock and then drove up the western shore of Priest Lake and climbed a handful of stellar routes on the Granite Pass Crag before car camping off a nearby Forest Service road. Such a trip is recommended for those who have climbed everything there is to climb in North Idaho and want to experience a new, very attractive area with a handful of fun climbs and absolutely no people, except the occasional vehicle or dirt bike blasting past on the road below.

Getting There/Approach

From the town of Priest River, Idaho, follow Highway 57 for about 50 miles, passing through the township of Nordman. Just past the turn-off to the Roosevelt Cedars, the road passes directly by a small crag located on the east side of the road. If you get to the actual Granite Pass junction, you have gone too far; turn around and proceed about a mile or so back to the roadside crag. The approach to the crag takes less than two seconds. It is also possible to walk back south along the road and locate a patch of rock slabs set back among the trees. A few top rope anchors are located on this crag, but grades and quality are unknown.

Appendix 1

Who to Contact for Recreation Information

Federal Agencies

Idaho Panhandle National Forests
Supervisor's Office
3815 Schreiber Way
Coeur d'Alene, ID 83815
www.fs.fed.us/ipnf
(208) 765-7223

Priest Lake Ranger District
32203 Highway 57
Priest River, ID 83856
http://www.fs.fed.us/ipnf/priestlake/
(208) 443-2512

Bonners Ferry Ranger District
6286 Main St.
Bonners Ferry, ID 83805
http://www.fs.fed.us/ipnf/bonnersferry/
(208) 267-5561

Sandpoint Ranger District
1500 Highway 2, Suite 110
Sandpoint, ID 83864
http://www.fs.fed.us/ipnf/sandpoint/
(208) 263-5111

Kootenai National Forest
Supervisor's Office
1101 U.S. Highway 2 West
Libby, MT 59923
www.fs.fed.us/r1/kootenai
(406) 293-6211

Three Rivers Ranger District
Troy Ranger Station
1437 North Highway 2
Troy, MT 59935
(406) 295-4693

Libby Ranger District
Canoe Gulch Ranger Station
12557 Highway 37 North
Libby, MT 59923
(406) 293-7773

Cabinet Ranger District
2693 Highway 200
Trout Creek, MT 59874
(406) 827-3533

State Agencies
Idaho Department of Lands
Priest Lake Supervisory Area
4053 Cavanaugh Bay Road
Coolin, ID 83821
(208) 443-2516

Idaho Department of Lands
Pend Oreille Supervisory Area
2550 Highway 2 West
Sandpoint, ID 83864
(208) 263-5104

Recreation Group
Spokane Mountaineers
P.O. Box 1013
Spokane, WA 99210-1013
(509) 838-4974
www.spokanemountaineers.org

Appendix 2

The Seven Principles of "Leave No Trace"

"Leave No Trace" is a nationally recognized outdoor educational and ethical program. The seven principles of Leave No Trace are not laws or rules; they are guidelines to follow when visiting remote backcountry areas. One poorly located campsite or campfire may seem insignificant, but thousands of such instances over time will seriously degrade the outdoor experience for all. Leaving no trace is everyone's responsibility.

1) Plan Ahead and Prepare

Know the regulations and special concerns for the area you'll visit. Prepare for extreme weather, hazards and emergencies. Schedule your trip to avoid times of high use. Visit in small groups. Split larger parties into groups of four to six. Repackage food to minimize waste. Use a map and compass to eliminate the use of marking paint, rock cairns or flagging.

2) Travel and Camp on Durable Surfaces

Durable surfaces include established trails and campsites, rock, gravel, dry grasses or snow. Protect riparian areas by camping at least 200 feet from lakes and streams. Good campsites are found, not made. Altering a site is not necessary. In popular areas: Concentrate use on existing trails and campsites; walk single file in the middle of the trail, even when wet or muddy; and keep campsites small. Focus activity in areas where vegetation is absent. In pristine areas: Disperse use to prevent the creation of campsites and trails; and avoid places where impacts are just beginning.

3) Dispose of Waste Properly

Pack it in, pack it out. Inspect your campsite and rest areas for trash or spilled foods. Pack out all trash, leftover food, and litter. Deposit solid human waste in catholes dug 6 to 8 inches deep at least 200 feet from water, camp and trails. Cover and disguise the cathole when finished. Pack out toilet paper and hygiene products. To wash yourself or your dishes, carry water 200 feet away from streams or lakes and use small amounts of biodegradable soap. Scatter strained dishwater.

4) Leave What You Find

Preserve the past: Examine, but do not touch cultural or historic structures and artifacts. Leave rocks, plants and other natural objects as you find them. Avoid introducing or transporting non-native species. Do not build structures, furniture or dig trenches.

5) Minimize Campfire Impacts

Campfires can cause lasting impacts to the backcountry. Use a lightweight stove for cooking and enjoy a candle lantern for light. Where fires are permitted, use established fire rings, fire pans or mound fires. Keep fires small. Only use sticks from the ground that can be broken by hand. Burn all wood and coals to ash, put out campfires completely, then scatter cool ashes.

6) Respect Wildlife

Observe wildlife from a distance. Do not follow or approach them. Never feed animals. Feeding wildlife damages their health, alters natural behaviors, and exposes them to predators and other dangers. Protect wildlife and your food by storing rations and trash securely. Control pets at all times, or leave them at home. Avoid wildlife during sensitive times: mating, nesting, raising young or during winter.

7) Be Considerate of Other Visitors

Respect other visitors and protect the quality of their experience. Be courteous. Yield to other users on the trail. Step to the downhill side of the trail when encountering pack stock. Take breaks and camp away from trails and other visitors. Let nature's sounds prevail. Avoid loud voices and noises.

For additional information, contact the Leave No Trace Center for Outdoor Ethics at (800) 332-4100 or look up www.lnt.org.

Glossary

anchor – the main point of protection used to safely belay or rappel from.

arête – a sheer, knife-edged sliver of rock generally formed by glaciers.

beer – favorite drink of most rock climbers. Often used synonymously with the words *water* or *food*.

belay – in a roped safety system, the belay is the *anchor* point where the rope is fed out, taken in or stopped to catch falls. A belayer is one who performs the act of belaying.

beta – an explanation of the sequence of specific climbing moves; often used in place of the word *information*.

Bombay chimney – a type of bottomless *chimney* that gives the climber a sense of standing over a Bombay door on a B-52 bomber

bouldering – climbing without ropes close to the ground.

bulge – a rounded portion of the rock that protrudes from a cliff side.

bulldogging – moving forward in a diligent manner.

buttress – a large, ridge-like portion of rock that protrudes from a mountain face.

cairn – a stack of rocks place on the ground by hikers or climbers to mark a particular trail or junction between trails.

cam – a type of *pro*.

chimney – a large crack in the rock that is big enough to fit your entire body into.

choss – unsavory rock; shattered, loose, possibly dangerous.

clip-in – to place a piece of climbing rope into an anchor system

corner – also known as a dihedral or open book, this is where two flat portions of rock meet to form a crease on a rock face.

couloir – French word describing a snow or ice gully.

cruxy – difficult, or, the most difficult portion of a particular climb

dihedral – see *corner*.

dike – a vein of hard rock (such as quartz) that protrudes from the cliff face.

down-climbing – to reverse upward rock climbing moves in an effort to safely descend, generally performed without use of a rope.

dyno sequence – to dynamically lunge for a particular hand hold.

fifth-class climbing – type of climbing where a fall would result in death.

fist crack – a crack roughly the size of one's fist.

flake – a sliver of rock that has been separated from the main rock face.

fourth-class climbing – climbing on large holds on steep rock. A fall may result in injury or death.

friction – pressing one's rock shoes flat against the rock.

Gaston or Gaston move – the act of pulling sideways on a handhold

gendarme – a tower-like chunk of rock usually found on a ridge crest and generally formed by glaciers.

hand crack – a crack that is the width of your hand.

handline – safety rope used to cross dangerous sections of rock.

headwall – a section of steep or perhaps vertical rock usually found just below the summit of an alpine peak.

hexentric – a type of *pro.*

in-cut – a hold you can get your fingers behind.

juggy – large, positive hand holds.

lieback – the act of climbing that involves pulling with the hands and pushing with the feet in opposition.

manky – unsafe, unsightly, crappy, useless.

massif – a cluster of alpine peaks generally formed around the same time due to the same geologic event

munge – mossy or wet

nubbin – a tiny piece of rock that protrudes from a cliff side.

onsight – climbing a route for the first time without any prior knowledge (or *beta*) about the climb.

off-width – a crack that is bigger than the size of a climber's hand but is not big enough to qualify as a *chimney.*

piton – a piece of shaped metal that is hammered into a crack and used as *pro.*

pro – short for protection, this refers to pieces of technical climbing gear used to protect a climber if they should fall from the rock.

pumpy – difficult or tiring.

redpoint – to lead a climb without falling, having first rehearsed the moves or perhaps *top roped* the climb.

roof – an overhanging section of rock.

runout – to climb so far past one's last piece of *pro* that a fall would probably result in injury or death.

simul-climbing – the process of two or more climbers moving together in tandem without stopping to *belay.*

slab – a section of rock that is less than vertical but steep enough to be climbed, often via *friction.*

sling – a piece of rope wrapped around rocks, trees or other natural objects to aid in the *belay* process or to form an *anchor.*

sloper – a smooth, downward facing chunk of rock.

smearing – see *friction.*

snow finger – a steep, thin snow gully or *couloir.*

stem – pressing both feet against opposite holds.

syncline – a geologic formation characterized by an S-shaped pattern in the rock.

TCU – stands for tri camming unit, a type of *pro.*

top rope – a roped safety system whereby a rope is dropped down from the top of a cliff and used to protect climbers against a fall.

trad – short for traditional, this refers to a style of rock climbing where the climber only uses non-permanent pieces of technical protection to ascend a climb (as opposed to bolts or other such permanent types of protection).

traverse – to move sideways during the act of rock climbing.

trending – moving toward.

trundling – to purposely knock rocks off a ledge or slope.

under-cling – the act of using fingers or hands to cling to an overhanging piece of rock while traversing directly out from under it and then continuing up the climb.

wafer flake – a very thin *flake.*

willywhack – bushes, weeds, bramble.

Index by route name

Index by rating

About the Author

Thaddeus Laird has traveled to five continents to quell his longtime climbing passions. Born in Honolulu, Hawaii, Laird's first lesson in climbing was trying to scale a Norfolk pine tree to "get a better view of the mountains." One concussion and a few stitches later, Laird had found his calling in life.

Promptly after graduation from high school, Laird moved to Colorado to pursue his dreams of becoming a ski bum. Here, he took his first rock climbing lessons and was soon spending every free minute clinging to the cliffs around Gunnison, Colorado. Laird later attended Western State College, in Gunnison, and received a Bachelor of Arts degree in outdoor education. He worked for several years as a mountaineering instructor for the Colorado Outward Bound School.

After college, Laird embarked on a one-year, around-the-world climbing epic funded by low-interest credit cards and the occasionally published outdoor article. Writing has always come naturally to Laird; his mother is a well-known children's book author in Hawaii.

In 2001, Laird moved to Sandpoint, Idaho, and soon found the area to be the perfect place to climb, ski and explore. After a brief stint in Berkeley, California, Laird returned to Sandpoint and somehow convinced Keokee Publishing to let him write a guidebook on climbing in the region; the first such guidebook written since 1987.

A freelance author and copywriter, Laird has had his articles published in *Mountainfreak, The Mountain Gazette, Mountainzone.com, Idaho Golf, Shift* and *Sandpoint Magazine*. He was published in a travel anthology titled "The Best Travel Writing of 2007." To read more of his work, look up www.thadlairdcreative.com.

Laird currently lives in Bend, Oregon, with the love of his life, Jessica, and her two Chihuahuas.

Other fine guidebooks published by Keokee Books

Trails of Wild Cabinets by Dennis Nicholls

Soft cover, 160 pages
ISBN 1-879628-22-8 $14

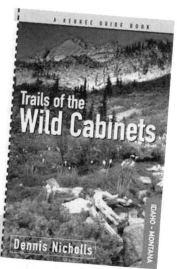

Sprawling across northern Idaho and north-western Montana, the Cabinet Mountains are one of the little-known ranges of the Rocky Mountains. Author Dennis Nicholls has penned the first-ever hiking and biking guide to the trails of this magnificent range. This guidebook includes descriptions of 82 trails, maps and photos, and a features chart to help readers more easily find trails with major points of interest such as lakes, waterfalls, old-growth forest, lookouts and peaks. Also included is a sketch of the natural history for the range and several essays drawn from Nicholls' own years of hiking in the Cabinets.

Trails of the Wild Selkirks by Dennis Nicholls

Soft cover, 336 pages
ISBN 1-879628-23-6 $16.50

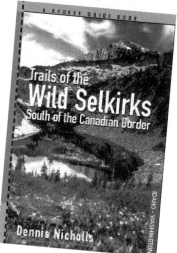

The Selkirk Mountains of northeastern Washington and northern Idaho hold a fantastic variety of landscapes, from lush rain forests to dry grasslands to the cirques and granite of its high peaks. This guidebook identifies trails suitable for mountain bikers and includes detailed descriptions of 107 trails, numerous maps and photos, an absorbing natural history for the range, and a features chart to help readers more easily find trails with major points of interest. An absorbing natural history for the range, along with several essays drawn from the author's own adventures are also provided.

On the Trail of the Ice Age Floods by Bruce Bjornstad

Soft cover, 320 pages
ISBN 978-1-879628-27-4 $19

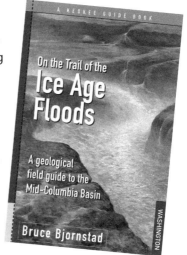

During the last great Ice Age some 15,000 years ago, the Pacific Northwest was repeatedly decimated by cataclysmic floods unlike anything of modern times. This guidebook explores the origins and mysteries of the great floods and describes in detail the 19 types geologic features they left behind. The hands-on field guide features 70 flood-formed sites, 30 hiking and biking trails, and seven driving and aerial tours in the Mid-Columbia Basin where one can witness the awesome power of the ancient floods.

Order online at www.keokeebooks.com or call 1-800-880-3573 Monday through Friday between 8:30 a.m. and 5:30 p.m. Pacific Time.

Notes

Notes

Notes

Notes

Notes